Victorian Antiques

Nathaniel Harris

 Golden Press

Published in 1973 by **Golden Press, New York,**
a division of Western Publishing Company Inc.
Library of Congress Catalog Card Number: 73–81305

Created, designed and produced for
Western Publishing Company Inc. by
Trewin Copplestone Publishing Ltd, London

Printed in Italy by
Officine Grafiche Arnoldo Mondadori, Verona
Filmset by Photoprint Plates Ltd, Rayleigh, Essex
World rights reserved by
Western Publishing Company, Inc.
GOLDEN and GOLDEN PRESS ® are trademarks
of Western Publishing Company Inc.

ISBN: 0 307 43114 2

Acknowledgements

The photographs for this book were taken by Michael
Dyer Associates except for those credited below to:
Bayou Bend Collection, Museum of Fine Arts,
Houston: 16; Birmingham Museum and Art Gallery:
17r; Geremy Butler: 23; Cooper-Bridgeman
Library: 1, 9t, 15, 18t, 34, 45b, 79; Country Life: 58;
Cutty Sark Society: 40; Doulton Group: 55, 56t;
Hamlyn Group: 21, 30b, 31, 71, 73; Metropolitan
Museum, New York: 59; National Army Museum,
London: 38; RIBA: 51; Sheffield Corporation: 17l;
Victoria and Albert Museum: 13t, 13b, 18b, 27, 28,
30t, 62, 64r, 67; Worshipful Company of Goldsmiths,
London: 26.
The Publishers also gratefully acknowledge:
Bethnal Green Museum: 4, 5, 11, 35, 36l, 44, 45t, 50,
60, 76, 77l; Cameo Corner, London: 24, 25b, 32b,
37, 47; Editions Graphiques Gallery, London: 68, 75;
Geffrye Museum, London: 6, 70; Richard Grosvenor
Antiques, London: 12, 13b; John Hall Antiques,
London: 39, 41, 43, 46, 49: Eleanor Hickox, Chelsea
Antique Market: 48; Kensington and Chelsea
Borough Corporation (Leighton House): 32t, 33,
54, 56b, 61t; Nerissa Knights, Chelsea Antique
Market: 7b, 10; Claire Leimbach: 77r; William
Morris Gallery, Walthamstow: 29b, 63, 72t, 74;
G. and C. Parry-Crooke: 3, 7t, 36r, 65, 69t; Purple
Shop, Antiquarius Market, London: 37, 78, 80;
Sotheby and Co., London: 14, 20, 25t; Stourbridge
Glass Museum: 23; Victoria and Albert Museum:
9b, 19, 29t, 53, 57, 61b, 66, 69b, 72b.

Contents

*Opposite An interesting collection which, among
other things, illustrates the range of materials
used by the Victorians: shell work (the box),
tortoiseshell and silver (opera glasses), gold
studded with turquoises (thimble).*

*Page 1 Coalport was one of the leading porcelain
manufacturers, specializing in Rococo. This is a
typical example, with flowers, gilding, skilful
moldings and a curving handle.*

Reminders of the Victorian past are all around us. When we visit the Houses of Parliament, the Statue of Liberty, the Paris Opera, we are in direct contact with Victorian dreams and ideals. 19th-century public buildings, monuments and bridges are common in most big cities, and many people still live in streets planned by Victorian architects – perhaps in the actual houses they built. Smaller Victorian objects are equally familiar. Antique shops and street markets are full of them (at prices that are still not astronomical despite their popularity), and often they are closer to hand than that – closer than we think. A look in the family attic can reveal treasures that our anti-Victorian fathers rejected without having the heart to throw out – not, most likely, fine silver or porcelain, but much that is just as interesting if not as valuable: an old kettle or rolling pin, a box with a sturdy lock and an inscription denoting proud ownership, faded brown postcards of forgotten beauties, or a book with engraved illustrations. Anything of this sort can be made the basis of a collection, and such material contacts bring to life a past that is already half known through the reminiscences of our grandparents. It is just because they are so accessible and familiar that Victorian antiques have a special appeal.

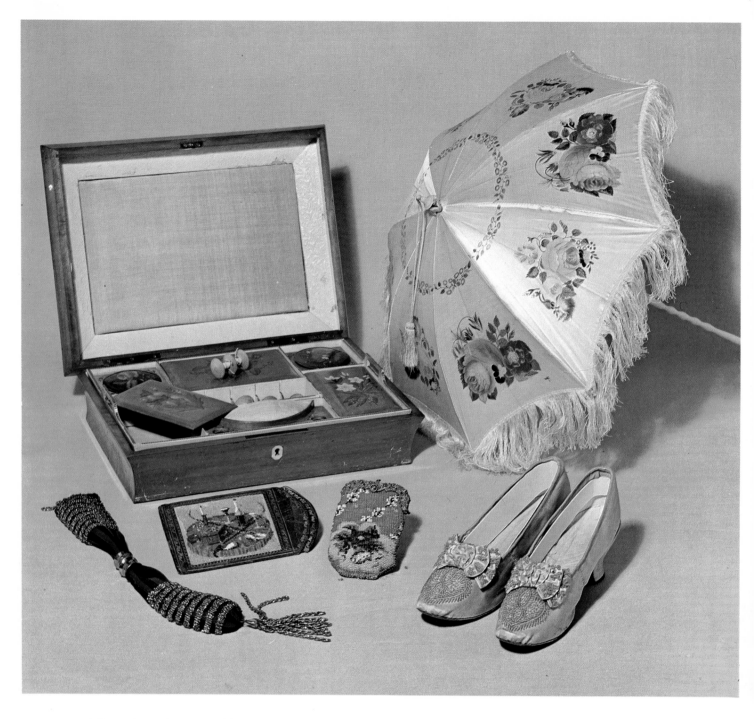

The Victorian World

IF you walk round a great museum like the Victoria and Albert Museum in London, entering the 19th-century rooms last of all, you feel as though you are passing from one world into another. The sheer quantity of the exhibits is greater and the range of styles wider than in, for example, the 18th-century rooms, and the 18th-century atmosphere of aristocratic elegance has entirely disappeared. A few exceptionally large and ugly exhibits will probably repel you at first. The unfavorable reaction wears off as you realize how much variety and vigor there is in the other pieces, but the sense of difference remains. There are machine-made objects here as well as works from the hands of craftsmen, cheap popular wares and imitations as well as display pieces, and experiments and novelties in plenty. Many items, worn with long use but obviously carefully looked after, suggest a thrifty domesticity rather than aristocratic negligence. Facts such as these contribute to the distinctive flavor of Victorian antiques. If we want to understand them properly we must delve a little into the world that gave birth to them, and try to understand why it was so different from all worlds before it.

Everybody associates the Victorians with the Industrial Revolution. In fact the idea has become such a cliché that it is now hard to appreciate just how revolutionary the period

Opposite *Delicate things for the delicate Victorian lady. A satinwood workbox, carriage parasol, beadbag, cardcase, purse, and satin shoes embroidered with amber colored glass beads.*

Below *The parlor was full of knick-knacks and rich materials. A doll's house like the one here faithfully copies the proportions and furnishings of the real thing.*

was. For all its sophistication, the 18th century was not so very different from the New Stone Age: most men lived and worked on the land, and ownership of land was the main source of power and wealth. Then, within a few decades, everything began to change. A soaring population crowded into sprawling towns that had shortly before been villages. The age of factories, shops, offices and warehouses, slums and railways, began in a great outburst of energy and squalor. By the time Queen Victoria came to the throne in 1837 the transformation was visibly under way; by the middle years of her reign Britain had become the "Workshop of the World" – a new kind of society, wealthier than any other in history, exporting vast quantities of goods,

and as yet unchallenged by rivals. Nothing like it had ever happened before, and the novelty of their situation partly accounts for the Victorian mood, with its peculiar mixture of exultation and uncertainty. Long before Queen Victoria's death in 1901, however, the United States and Germany had become industrial nations in which similarly Victorian attitudes prevailed.

These attitudes were essentially those of the middle class – the puritan ethic of hard work, domesticity and respectability. The middle class benefited most from the Industrial Revolution and increasingly set the tone of society. As before, the upper class lived in grand houses with attendant carriages, butlers, footmen and grooms; but the sons and daughters of

debauched Regency bucks now tended to adopt middle-class manners and morals. So did the respectable working class; only the illiterate and poverty-stricken masses below them knew nothing of strict morals and stern duty. The accession of the young queen, and her model married life with Prince Albert, symbolized a new era which had in reality begun some years before.

What sort of people made up the middle class? The question is worth asking, for they were the chief customers in the mass market for furniture, fabrics, glass and other household goods. This means that there were large numbers of them—perhaps getting on for a million—and that they could not all have been bankers and industrialists. An average middle-class mid-Victorian might be described as follows: he is a merchant in a small way of business or, even more likely, a clerk—not one of Charles Dickens's feckless young men beginning on ten shillings a week, but a trusted employee in middle life who earns between three and five hundred pounds a

year. He has saved hard in order to set up a home, and perhaps married late and/or prudently. He and his rapidly growing family live in a terraced house or in one of the newly popular semi-detached houses. They are by no means well off. The situation of the poor middle-class family is discussed in journals such as the *Englishwoman's Domestic Magazine*, which in 1859 asked "Can one live on £300 a-year?". The article encourages bachelor gentlemen and maiden ladies to marry and raise a family on such an income, but leaves them in no doubt that theirs will be a "frugal marriage". What the article does not mention is that they could expect to become more affluent in the years ahead, but could never be completely secure: bankruptcy and unemployment were always possibilities in an age of fierce competition, and if the wage-earner was ill or died there were no welfare benefits to prevent the family from sliding into the ranks of the desperate poor. Such people had only a precarious foothold above the seething world of dirt, darkness and violence; to slip into that world, as Dickens's characters, Oliver Twist and the Dorrit family did, was the Victorian nightmare.

The insecurity of life accounts for many features of the Victorian home. Home was the Englishman's castle, and also his shelter and retreat. The parlor, crammed with well-upholstered furniture, draperies, pictures and knick-knacks of every sort, satisfied his passion for display and provided the enclosed, secure atmosphere he craved. A good deal of the clutter was "ladies' work" done by the wife and daughters, who could not shame the breadwinner by working for money, but could not be allowed to remain sinfully idle. For those who could afford it, the dining room was also a display item, with sideboards loaded down with crockery, glass or silver. And for the master there was a study furnished in a heavier masculine style with a massive desk and deep armchairs. Even the bedroom was imposing, though the effect of a big four-poster would probably be softened by plush, curvaceous "French" furniture. The whole mass of family possessions would have been unmanageable without domestic servants, and it comes as something of a surprise to realize that even the less affluent middle class could afford them: the combined cost of a housemaid and cook was about £30 a year, only ten per cent of our "frugal" couple's income.

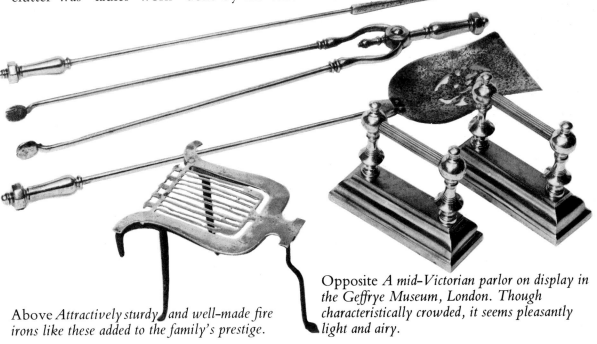

Above *Attractively sturdy and well-made fire irons like these added to the family's prestige.*

Opposite *A mid-Victorian parlor on display in the Geffrye Museum, London. Though characteristically crowded, it seems pleasantly light and airy.*

ENGLAND'S ROYAL SAILOR

H.R.H. Prince Alfred Ernest Albert

MESSRS. DALTON & BARTON MAN'FRS

Taste and economics interlocked in various other ways. Unlike aristocrats of the 18th-century the middle-class Victorian could not afford to have his furnishings specially made. Instead, he chose them from a range of mass-produced goods in a store. This meant that the responsibility for designing the product passed to the manufacturer, who of course preferred to turn out standardized designs for the largest possible market, concentrating on those that sold best and changing styles only very reluctantly. But there is no reason to suppose that the Victorian customer was dissatisfied with what he got: if a good many designs were bad or unoriginal, the fault lay in the taste of a whole class.

In the light of what we know about the middle class, Victorian taste becomes easier to understand. The middle-class householder admired and respected culture but, lacking the advantages of the 18th-century aristocrat, did not know enough about it to develop his own taste. One answer was to play safe and buy goods in styles that carried the authority of the past, whether ancient Greek or 18th-century. Another was to choose objects with

reassuringly realistic decoration that either copied nature or showed a picture; what was real could hardly be bad. A mass of decoration seemed another guarantee of artistic worth. In fact most Victorians identified decoration with beauty, failing to realize that a beautiful object must above all be well-proportioned, and that interesting textures are often more satisfying than applied decoration. But in 1851 the more intricate the ornamental decoration, the better people liked it.

1851 was the date of the Great Exhibition, held in London to celebrate and show off the supremacy of British manufactured goods in the specially constructed Crystal Palace. Here the overwhelming majority of the applied arts exhibitions were hideous–more so than their everyday equivalents, for as display pieces they were buried under elaborate decoration and made so huge as to be useless to anybody but a particularly tasteless giant. To cite and illustrate them is in a way unfair to the Victorians (though quite irresistible), but they do introduce us to the very worst in contemporary taste–the kind of experience that is best got over and done with.

Below *Kitchenware was doubtless less practical in Victorian times but forms an attractive range of "collectables".*

Opposite *Bentwood furniture made by the Viennese firm of Michael Thonet. The chairs have cane seats. This is perhaps the finest and most functional furniture of the mid–19th century.*

That there was another side of the matter, even in 1851, is shown by the bentwood chairs in the same exhibition. Made by bending the wood under steam, the resulting pieces were pleasingly light, elegant and useful objects in which decoration and design were one and the same thing–the patterned curves of the bent wood rods and struts. Bentwood furniture was manufactured in Vienna by Michael Thonet, and it says a good deal for the Victorians that they imported it in huge quantities throughout the 19th-century.

Few drawing-room items were so practical and simple; even pianos sometimes looked like tropical plants, overgrown with shaggy

masses of carved wooden leaves. The main exceptions, like bentwood chairs, were for use in the kitchen, or in the still numerous country cottages. The sound and roomy pinewood dresser was a piece of standard kitchen furniture that appeals strongly to modern taste–so much so that it is not only a collectors' item but is also made by present-day manufacturers. Dressers, tables and cupboards have the same down-to-earth, well-scrubbed appearance. And the gleaming copper pans and kettles, kitchen knives, rolling pins, jars, bowls, and moulds all have the kind of solid charm that comes from repeated use. In some of the furniture, traditional designs lived on into the 19th century–in such sturdy pieces as the rush-seated chair and the venerable Windsor chair, with its curved back of angled spokes. This "cottage"

tradition was, as we shall see, later to be a source of inspiration for attempts to reform Victorian design. Many other items made for use rather than show (brass fittings, gas lamps, oil lamps) have the same toughness and practicality. This is also true of relics from shops, public houses and railway stations. On these things the decoration is often the more charming because it is subservient to the function of the object—though there are always exceptions such as the many stoves that resemble miniature palaces, which must have been delightful but dangerous for children.

Critics of Victorian design—and there were many of them in the Victorian period—tended to lay the blame for its defects on machine production and the decline of the craftsman. Like so many sweeping statements, this contains a grain of truth but wildly exaggerates

the case. Machines played only a subordinate part in most of the trades that concern us, and where the workmanship was shoddy the fault lay just as often in mechanically repeated craft work; the carver crudely hacking out a set design probably produced as much bad furniture as the new carving machines. Even so, the quality of Victorian craftsmanship is generally excellent, and often better than that of previous centuries. The Great Exhibition pieces may be grotesque, but they are marvels of skill and ingenuity, while Victorian copies of earlier works are easy for an expert to spot because they are so much better made than the originals. When we recall that there had never before been such a huge demand for furniture, glass and pottery, we can hardly fail to be impressed by the high standard reached by most of it.

Something that is often overlooked is the sheer inventiveness that went into creating a great deal of Victoriana. Borne on by the tide of industrial expansion, the Victorians constantly experimented with new materials and techniques. Any kind of novelty or gadget found a ready market. These ranged from practical and ingenious "patent" furniture like iron and brass bedsteads to fanciful mid-century sofas with compartmentalized seats.

One of the most curious materials, developed though not invented in the 19th century, was papier mâché. In the 18th century, pulped and moulded paper had been used to make small domestic objects such as tea caddies and music racks. The Victorians extended its use to furniture, even applying it to wooden or metal frames to create papier mâché beds. At their best these papier mâché products are light and curvacious, with delicate painted or shell-inlay decoration. More im-

posing pieces, such as the prie-dieu – on which the Victorian paterfamilias knelt to pray, resting his knees on the seat and his elbows on the well-padded rail at the top – are perhaps not faultless designs, but have an unmistakable period charm.

A more solemn purpose was served by the new parian porcelain, so called because it resembled the Parian marble used to make many ancient Greek statues. This made it an ideal material for making replicas of such works, and hundreds of thousands of parian statuettes must have been produced during the Victorian period: famous antique statues, characters from Shakespeare, busts of contemporaries such as the Queen and General Gordon. And before we sneer at the Victorian taste for "culture on the mantelpiece", let us remember the reproduction paintings on our own walls, which amount to much the same thing.

Other inventions helped to bring art into the home more cheaply and efficiently. One was almost symbolic of the Age of Iron and Steel: the copper plates used for centuries to print engravings were replaced by more durable plates made of steel. Even cheaper and simpler was lithography, a colour printing process, famous because it was used by the French artists Toulouse-Lautrec and Bonnard. Interest in contemporary scenes and headline-making events was satisfied above all by Nathaniel Currier and James Merrit Ives, whose lithograph prints comprise an unrivalled record of American life in the second half of the 19th century.

The invention of photography was even more revolutionary in the long run. Today it is both an art form and a quick, simple, cheap way of capturing reality that is available to all of us. Its very accuracy has encouraged painters and other artists to abandon the old photographic realism and produce the kind of modern art that baffled the general public for so many years. But in the Victorian period photography was still a laborious and expensive pursuit that required elaborate equipment. Most pictures could only be taken after extended sittings, and it was the photographer who was tempted to imitate the poses and effects of paintings. Despite these limitations, surprisingly natural-looking portraits were produced, as well as contemporary scenes of great historical interest. There are Crimean War photographs dating from the 1850s, and Matthew Brady left a particularly moving record of the American Civil War.

Other developments had more immediate effects on style and fashion. In the early 19th century, the most prestigious glassware was cut crystal, facetted, transparent and gleaming like the diamonds that were the favored ornaments of the rich. As we might expect, cut glass was grandiosely represented at the Great Exhibition, by an enormous fountain made by Osler's of Wakefield. Shortly after the Exhibition, cut glass was completely eclipsed by the American invention of pressed glass. In the press-moulding process, machines were used to mould both the outside and the inside of glassware and bottles, creating quite complex relief patterns at a fraction of the cost of blown or cut ware. In the USA pressed glass was made in a lacy style with areas of raised dots and other decoration, but in Britain it was mainly used to imitate cut glass –

and so successfully that cut glass itself lost its snob value and went out of fashion for thirty years.

Inventions of this kind allowed thousands of middle-class people to indulge in modest domestic display. Silver, for example, remained the prerogative of the rich despite the introduction of mass-production techniques; but from the 1840s electroplated versions of silver centerpieces, vases and trophies were on sale at home and abroad. Electroplating involved the use of an electric current to coat a finished base metal object, usually made of a nickel alloy, with a thin sheet of silver or gold. Electroplate could be made from the same moulds as silver objects, and the nickel body sufficiently resembled silver to disguise the effects of wear and tear – two advantages not possessed by the older

copper-bodied Sheffield plate, which was rapidly driven out of production. The firm that patented electroplating, Elkington's of Birmingham, built up one of the great 19th-century businesses. Their reputation was such that they were allowed to make electroplated reproductions of many works of art in England and on the Continent.

Electroplating was also used to make inexpensive jewelry with a gold or silver finish. And the existence of a middle-class market brought into fashion a whole range of semi-precious stones such as amethyst, coral, topaz, opal, peridot, cornelian and lapis lazuli. There were also very cheap processes for manufacturing imitation jewelry that even the working classes could afford. Electro-gilding largely replaced the old pinchbeck imitation of gold, and designs were standard-ized in the interests of cheapness by die-stamping. Diamond substitutes, known in the 18th century, were now mass-produced; the most important were paste, which is basically high-quality glass, and marcasite, made from iron pyrites.

These imitations and substitutes were by no means "cheap and nasty": like almost all products produced in the Victorian age they were intended to last. And they were of great social importance in bringing a large section of the population into contact with refinements previously known only to the very rich. The boldness and originality of the manufacturing processes used are in sharp contrast to the styles in which the products were designed, deriving as they did almost exclusively from the great styles of the immediate past.

The lure of the past

IN most ages there have been one, or at most two, prevailing styles in the arts. The late 17th century, for example, was dominated by the Baroque style, and the early 18th by the Rococo. But there was no distinctive Victorian style until the emergence of Art Nouveau, right at the end of the period. Instead, the Victorians revived almost all the past styles they knew about—even the ancient Assyrian—and used them to decorate themselves and their possessions. Their omnivorous appetite for the historical will become obvious in the following pages, where we shall come across Greek-style furniture, Roman-style cameos, Renaissance-style pottery and Gothic-style jewelry. Even would-be reformers were so influenced by the prevailing atmosphere that they were more concerned with authenticity than with creating a new style. And much the same is true of the rest of Europe and also of the USA, which imported large quantities of goods from Britain.

In Britain itself this "historicizing" was at its height from roughly 1830 to 1860, but it was an extremely powerful influence all

A romantic view of the Middle Ages was typical of the 19th century as shown in the Spirit of Chivalry *by Maclise.*

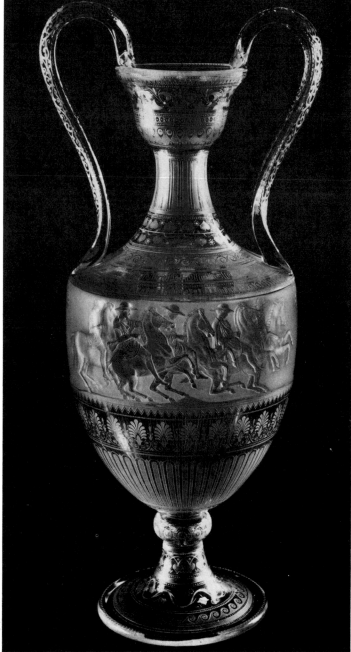

The "Elgin Vase" by John Northwood Senior—a glass version of a Greek pottery vase.

through the 19th century. A particular historical style might become high fashion for a time before being supplanted by something else, but it usually continued to find favor with a substantial section of the public. The products themselves ranged from direct imitations to more or less tasteful adaptations, the most fanciful being vaguely in the spirit of some past age. Apart from the inevitable examples of sheer bad taste, the least satisfactory productions were those in which the designer blithely applied a traditional design to a material for which it was never intended. Even a magnificent piece of glassware like the "Elgin" vase, with its lovely Greek shape and engraved decoration, is somehow disturbing just because it is glass and not, like the original, pottery. The idea that a design can be used on any kind of material was one of the most unfortunate of Victorian convictions.

But we must not forget that most of these "historical" items were soundly made, and that many of them were beautiful. Their dependence on past styles is a fact that we must appreciate if we are to understand them, but there is no reason why it should spoil our enjoyment of either the more bizarre or the really high-quality pieces.

Survivals and revivals: 18th-century styles

There was already a Victorian atmosphere about furniture made ten or fifteen years before the young queen came to the throne. The Regency style, with its roots in the 18th century, remained popular into the middle of the 19th, though it was now known as "Grecian" or "Antique"; but even in the 1820s it was becoming heavier and fuller – settling down, so to speak, like a reformed old rake. Elegance was sacrificed to a general rounding off of lines and angles, and seats were heavily padded with upholstery. Inevitably, the amount of applied ornament increased, and the typical Antique acanthus leaves and scrolls became more prominent. But restraint was rarely abandoned completely (perhaps only because of the conservatism of manufacturers), and Grecian is to people with sober tastes the most attractive early Victorian furniture.

The tendency to heaviness occurred because furniture could be made more comfortable than ever before. The familiar coiled spring (all too familiar to anyone who has slept on an old bed) was introduced in the 1820s, just at a time when fabrics were becoming cheaper. Not surprisingly, there was a vogue for well-upholstered furniture. But here, as so often, the innovation reflected the current mood rather than created it. One gets the impression that weightiness had a moral value for the early Victorians, as if it were a way of asserting that they were more in

earnest than the men of the 18th century and the Regency period. Even their cut glass carries the same message: the stems of glasses are much shorter and the decanters become more barrel-shaped (usually with large, top-heavy stoppers), giving way by the 1850s to flattened globe shapes with even lower centers of gravity.

The light, curvaceous Rococo style also carried over into the Victorian period, though it lost some of its sprightliness. In porcelain, Rococo was the single dominant influence throughout the 19th century. The wares produced at Sèvres in France had acquired immense prestige early in the century when they were collected by the Prince Regent and Beau Brummell, and vast quantities of imitation Sèvres were manufactured; "Coalport Sèvres" is probably best known, but Minton's and the Worcester Royal Porcelain Company also produced Sèvres, as well as wares in the styles of other 18th-century porcelain factories such as Meissen and Chelsea. The standard of execution was very high indeed, and many of the direct imitations are almost indistinguishable from their originals. Any Victorian suspicion of 18th-century frivolity in the Rococo was evidently disarmed by its naturalistic qualities and wealth of decoration—encrusted shells, leaves and bouquets of flowers, pierced work (especially on the edges of plates), brightly painted colours and luxurious gilding. Rococo was popular for early Victorian jewelry settings, and also for silver, but in a more generalized way; flowers, fruit and other naturalistic decoration are more in evidence than Rococo curves.

The opposite is true of "Louis XIV furniture", which one contemporary authority, J. C. Loudon, primly described as having "curved lines and excess of curvilinear ornament"—scrolls, shell ornaments, and cabriole

legs with curving knees. The style was introduced in the 1820s and, despite the disapproval of Loudon and other pundits, soon rivalled Grecian in popularity. The disapproval was moral rather than artistic: Louis XIV – we should call it Louis XV – was frivolous, French and feminine, three terms that were rapidly becoming synonymous in Victorian England. It is the most comfortably luxurious Victorian furniture, tempting for the parlor and almost irresistible as bedroom furniture.

The rounding off of lines and angles gave rise to a new type of chair, and one so popular that it deserves separate mention. This was the graphically named balloon-back, which seems to have evolved from the right-angled Grecian chair but often shows affinities with Louis XIV style. You can find versions in different woods, upholstered or with cane seats, with straight turned legs or cabriole legs: the balloon-back was a multi-purpose design, and during its great vogue could be found in several rooms of the Victorian house.

Later in the century, some of these styles came into fashion for a second time, and there were also versions of previously unrevived 18th-century styles. Some of them represent a striving for simplicity, induced by the criticisms directed against the Victorian passion for elaborate decoration. In the 1860s silver designs were often inspired by the works of Robert Adam, the Scottish Neo-classical interior decorator, and by the earlier and still plainer Queen Anne style. There was also an Adam revival in furniture, and an Adam satinwood cabinet by Wright and Mansfield won a prize at the Paris Exhibition of 1867. But as always in the Victorian period, there was a countertrend too. Late 18th-century French furniture (Louis XVI), made in exotic woods and decorated with marquetry, ormolu and porcelain plaques, came into fashion at roughly the same time as the restrained Adam pieces. Finally, at the end of the century there was a vogue for reproductions of classic English furniture (Chippendale, Hepplewhite, Sheraton). In the use of 18th-century styles at least, the wheel had come almost full circle.

21

A typical jardinière of the Victorian period made of pottery and painted in deep, rich colors.

Greek and Roman Styles

For hundreds of years, ancient Greece and Rome had a prestige among Europeans that is now hard for us to imagine. From the Italian Renaissance to the beginning of the 20th century, classical literature and history provided models of style and conduct, and Victorian public school boys still studied more Latin and Greek than English. And although creatively developed, all decorative styles since the Renaissance were ultimately derived from classical antiquity. To draw directly upon it was to be cloaked with unchallengeable dignity and authority. Even eroticism, otherwise publicly suppressed, could be indulged in without feelings of guilt if you lingered over Sir Lawrence Alma-Tadema's rosy nudes, wrapped in a romantic haze of flower petals and clothed in scanty "classical" draperies. Engraved prints were of course made of such academic paintings, and photographers also took the opportunity to make nude studies. It seems equally likely that the presence of nudes added a certain spice to the pictures and reliefs on pottery, glass, silver and other objects – though it would be simple-minded to think that respectable eroticism was the Victorians' sole interest in the Antique.

Classical subjects and decoration were used in all the applied arts. Only furniture was not directly imitated, no doubt because too little was known about the Greek and Roman originals. Even Grecian furniture represents no more than an evocation of the classical world with applied Greco-Roman ornament. Apart from statuary, reproduced in miniature in bronze, brass, parian ware and spelter (zinc), the most popular model was Greek pottery, which the Victorians assiduously copied and translated into other materials. The so-called Etruscan ware of the 19th century was in fact based on the Greek red-figure style, with backgrounds painted black around unpainted figures left in the original red of the earthenware. Etruscan ware was made from terracotta, which was also used for vases and mugs with relief decoration, and for garden statuary; and terracotta plaques were put up on the walls or incorporated in them. On a less ambitiously academic level there were the many plates and other wares painted with romanticized pastoral scenes.

Greek pottery styles were imitated for silver and electroplated tableware. The decoration is generally restrained, but there is the usual mid-century leaning towards dumpiness. Tea and coffee pots were based on a Greek vase type with three lips, a handle and a shaped foot. Exactly the same design was produced in crystal glass with engraved decoration, though most makers used paint or colored glass to approximate more closely to the "body" of Greek pottery. Opaline glass – either white opal or the greyish alabaster glass – was most common, with painted friezes and scenes, and there are also splendid objects in black glass, painted in red and black to

Cameo glass was made by cutting away a white overlay, an exacting and expensive technique. This vase is by Thomas Webb and sons.

their Greek prototypes—a fact that makes them more, not less, interesting than straightforward earthenware imitations.

Two techniques that we associate with Roman jewelry were developed in late Victorian glass. Intaglio work, which involves cutting the design into the material, was essentially a variation on cutting or deep engraving. But cameo glass, in which the design stands out in white against a coloured ground, was a technical feat of the first order. True cameo jewelry was created by cutting into precious or semi-precious stones, but there were also cameos made from mollusk shells which were imported in quantities from Italy and then mounted and set in England. The vogue of mosaic jewelry, also made abroad, was great but short-lived, expiring by about the middle of the century.

The classical style was bound to command the respect and admiration of the Victorians, but their interest was reinforced by contemporary events. The abortive Roman Republic, set up by Garibaldi and Mazzini in 1850, may have had some influence. Certainly Garibaldi, liberator of Italy, became a popular hero in England. Probably more important was the scientific excavation of Pompeii, the Roman town destroyed by an eruption of Vesuvius in AD 79. 19th-century archaeology provided the first concrete picture of daily life in the Roman Empire, and unearthed new designs that could be copied or adapted. On a lighter note, there is "Roman" jewelry made of lava and mounted in gold—a typical expression of Victorian fantasy, and a rather touching tribute from one age to another.

Renaissance styles

The Italian Renaissance began in the 14th and lasted until the end of the 16th century, spreading into France at the end of the period and influencing the rest of Europe in a less direct way. It was partly a revival of Greco-Roman culture and partly a new outburst of artistic creativity. Victorian manufacturers and craftsmen had no inhibitions about copying directly from antiquity, and were therefore more concerned with the less imitative aspects of Renaissance art—though there are interesting Victorian cameos and other objects that can be called copies of copies (or at least adaptations of adaptations), the Roman, Renaissance and Victorian pieces being strikingly similar though subtly different in mood.

The Roman-style architecture of the Renaissance, with its round arches and supporting

resemble red-figure ware. No technical virtuosity can make a smooth, gleaming, obviously brittle material like glass resemble the rough, tough look of pottery. Most of these pieces have a gentler, more romantic aura than

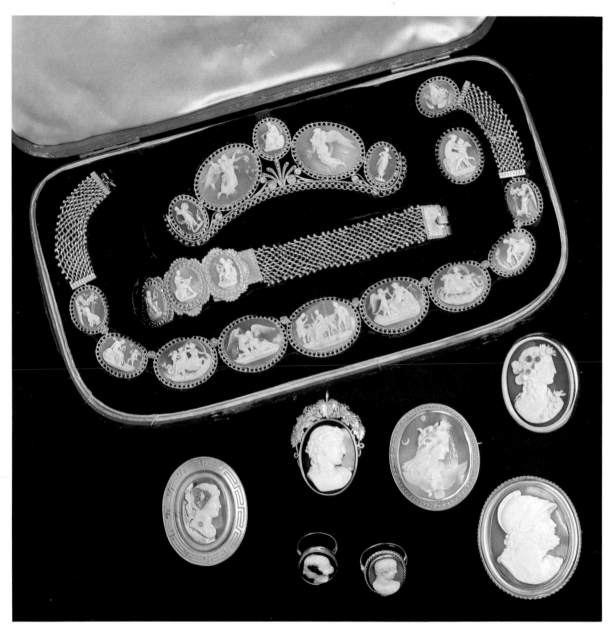

columns, was often used decoratively for objects such as stoves and clocks, which could be effectively framed. The same building-like effect is created by the "Free Renaissance" furniture of the late 19th century, for example in massive two-story bookcases with two sets of columns rising up to a cornice with a fanciful pediment. This style was a tremendous commercial success from the 1870s, and its heavy, foursquare quality looks like a deliberate reassertion of the Victorian taste for mass and detail. The carving and inlay work on Free Renaissance furniture is often superb, but its distinctive feature is the great number of shelves, brackets and cupboards it carried. The irreverent thought comes to mind that the mania for accumulation that filled the parlor may have been getting out of hand . . .

Pottery was even more strongly influenced by Renaissance styles. Italian maiolica ware, painted in stunning blues and yellows, was copied (as Majolica) by Minton's in particular.

This group contains lava jewelry, mosaic work, and an Etruscan

pe bracelet.

But unlike the Italians, Minton's artists rarely painted over the glaze, and the copies lack the pleasing matt-textured appearance of the originals. Another type of Majolica that may delicately be called a matter of taste is in imitation of Della Robbia pottery, usually with a relief design of leaves covered with a green glaze. The French Renaissance was also a source for pottery styles (it contributed something to Free Renaissance furniture too), though the result tended to be technically impressive rather than elegant in any way. Palissy ware, famous for its high relief decoration of insects and plants, inspired the Victorian potter to new heights of ornamental excess; at last almost anything with relief decoration was called Palissy ware. Henri II or St Porchaire pottery was equally impressive, with sophisticated patterns of colored clays inlaid in a buff body, but unfortunately the pot itself is all too often a heavy, lumpish object.

For display pieces in metal, makers sought
inspiration in the works of Benvenuto Cellini,
the master goldsmith of his age, and author
of a racy, boastful autobiography that still
makes marvelous reading. Cellini was a man
of the late Renaissance or Mannerist period,
when the great artists like Michelangelo
seemed to have exhausted the possibilities of
art, and all that was left to others was to
develop virtuoso skills to their furthest extent.
Cellini's incredibly detailed patterns of gods
and goddesses, mythical beasts, cherubs, arabesques and festoons were copied by Victorians
on to ewers, vases, dishes and trays, as well as
a number of smaller objects. Electroplate
and spelter were produced in the same style
for people who could not afford silver, and
Cellini ewers were even made in porcelain.

Cameos and other forms of jewelry in the
Renaissance style were popular in the mid-
Victorian period, many of them being exact
reproductions of the original pieces. There is
more life, however, in the pieces designed a
few years later by C. R. Ashbee, who swam
against the stream in creating magnificent
settings in a period when most jewelers were
concerned only to show off the stones.

Glass was less influenced by Renaissance
styles, though arabesques and other details
were occasionally used. A good many glasses
have affinities with the famous Venetian
wares of the 16th century, with trailed
decoration, convoluted stems or colored glass
canes embedded in the body; but the resem-
blance remains rather loose. In fact, with the
exception of Greek pottery, historical styles
seem to have influenced glass less than any of
the other applied arts.

The Elizabethan style
In Victorian eyes the Elizabethan style had
many advantages. The fact that it was a
national style made it seem somehow more
authentic than revived styles taken from other
lands, and its very name linked it with a
time of English greatness and expansion. There
is a certain irony in this, for the style was in
fact based upon English furniture designs of
the Stuart period, which was far from glorious.
Nevertheless the appeal to Anglo-Saxon sentiment worked, and proved equally effective in
America, where this "old English" or
"colonial" style was if anything still more
popular. It was solid and imposing, and ornate
but not frivolous. The tall rectangular back of
the Elizabethan chair could take spiral up-
rights, a padded and embroidered back and a

crest at the top with no loss of dignity; and the massive Elizabethan table, dripping with tendril-like strapwork carving, remained an assertively masculine-looking object. With such furniture in his library, the Victorian paterfamilias could imagine himself a bold baron in his hall—a private fantasy that was undoubtedly common in an age so impressed by the novels of Sir Walter Scott. In fact the typical Elizabethan chair was often called an "Abbotsford" after Scott's house, itself partly decorated in Elizabethan style. If he could afford it, our paterfamilias had silver on his table that was made in a sympathetic style, with the same rigid structure covered with strapwork or naturalistic ornament.

Other Elizabethan pieces, particularly hall furniture such as benches, evoke a ruder and more spacious age even more forcibly. If the Elizabethan style failed to dominate the Victorian age it was because there was another national style with an even wider and stronger emotional appeal: the Gothic.

Romanticism and reform: the Gothic style
Strange as it may seem, the Victorians were obsessively interested in the Middle Ages. This period, long despised by Englishmen as barbarous and wild, now became a repository for all kinds of emotions. To those who were horrified by the noise and dirt of 19th-century cities, it represented a green and pleasant "Merrie England". To men attracted

Opposite *Elizabethan-style silver candelabrum. The Victorians enjoyed the florid dignity of this style. Notice the "Celliniesque" decoration of leaves and scrolls.*

Left *This gilt chair, made around 1825–30, is an early example of Victorian Gothic furniture. The medieval inspiration is rather vague.*

27

A. W. N. Pugin was one of the pioneers of serious Victorian Gothic. The necklace and cross were designed by him in about 1848, and are set with garnets and pearls.

by the new High Church movement it was a model Age of Faith. And to ordinary people it was the Age of Chivalry, providing an escape into the never-never land of knightly quests and maidens imprisoned in tall towers. These images were reinforced by literature of all sorts, from Scott's novels and Byron's dark heroes to Tennyson's *Lady of Shalott* and *Idylls of the King*. Serious painters like the Pre-Raphaelites tried to recapture the devotional mood of medieval art, while a host of more conventional artists and illustrators turned out chivalric-sentimental anecdotes.

The great medieval style in architecture and decoration was Gothic. This was the style of the great cathedrals (Chartres and Reims in France; Salisbury, Lincoln and Gloucester in England), and as such had the unmistakable stamp of high seriousness. The Gothic style was revived in architecture during the 18th century, and in the 19th received the highest official approval by being used for the Houses of Parliament. In the applied arts, and especially furniture, it was to be the most important

of the revival styles, favored by the ordinary customer because it was at once solid, romantic and ornamental, and by the avant-garde because, if properly made, it could possess the same qualities of honest craftsmanship as its medieval prototypes.

The only thing that restrained Victorian enthusiasm for Gothic was respect for its religious associations: there seemed to be a touch of blasphemy in applying the style to purely secular objects. In some crafts this objection held throughout the 19th century: Gothic embroidery was rare except for ecclesiastical vestments (vaguely medieval scenes hardly count), and almost all Gothic silver is ecclesiastical plate. In furniture, despite a slow start, the style had become established by the 1830s as a rival of Grecian, Louis XIV and Elizabethan; these were the "big four" of early Victorian furniture. At this time Gothic pieces were not imitations of medieval originals but standard 19th-century designs with carvings in the medieval style—spiky pinnacles, projecting leafy crockets, buttresses, tracery and so on.

Above *This design for a Gothic bookcase is from one of Pugin's books.*

Below *Pottery by the Martin brothers. The grotesque bird at the back typifies the "Gothic" side of their work.*

A more thoroughgoing attempt to revive genuine Gothic furniture was made by A. W. N. Pugin, who designed the Gothic decorative detail for the Houses of Parliament. Pugin was a devout Catholic as well as a medievalist, and his advocacy of Gothic in *Gothic Furniture in the Style of the Fifteenth Century* (1835) and *Contrasts* (1836) was based as much on religious as on artistic grounds. The artistic argument was that medieval craftsmanship was more honest because it revealed joints and other elements of the construction instead of covering them up. In following this medieval example Pugin was in fact anticipating later reformers and establishing one of the main principles of modern design. In addition to reproduction pieces he made a number of more original designs in which late Gothic naturalistic decoration was only a starting-point; and he also designed effective Gothic jewelry. The best of this was in cast iron, the heaviness of the metal setting off the intricacy of the designs, but Pugin also started a minor revival of the medieval art of enameling. Though he was a well-known public figure,

Pugin's influence was smaller and less happy than might have been expected – partly because he died in 1852, when he was only forty, and partly because it was his more elaborate and academic pieces, shown in the Medieval Court at the Great Exhibition, that caught the public fancy. For this reason Pugin's work has only been properly appreciated in recent years, and he is never likely to be as famous as later reformers like William Morris.

The Gothic, like the Greco-Roman and Renaissance, was an all-purpose style that was used on any number of things – on clocks, bird-cages and picture frames, metalwork and even pottery. The most interesting of this Gothic pottery was made by the three Martin brothers, who specialized in grotesques such as we can see on Gothic cathedrals, including weird animal figures and pots in the form of distorted human faces. The only art untouched by Gothic was porcelain: the Victorians, though not notable for their discretion in these matters, had more sense than to graft the rugged medieval forms on to the smooth hard surfaces of this material.

There is much more to be said about the Gothic revival, which was also the preferred style of design reformers and the more art-conscious section of the public. We shall be returning to the subject later in this book.

Top *Mid-century porcelain; Copeland ice pail, Worcester sugar bowl, and a plate, vase and ewer by Minton's.*

Left Bowl by the Martin brothers. *A pleasing, remarkably modern-looking work in its combination of rough and smooth features.*

Above Minister jug of white stoneware, made *around 1840 by Meigh of Hanley. An intimidatingly ecclesiastical piece of Gothic ware.*

Minor revival styles

We have now looked at the main historical styles. However, there were also many minor revivals, usually short-lived and sometimes confined to a single craft. Archaeological discoveries provided a rich field for exploitation. Shrewd manufacturers cashed in with "Trojan" designs suggested by Schliemann's finds, and after Layard's discoveries at Nineveh and Nimrud the human-headed winged bulls of Assyria enjoyed a brief vogue in jewelry.

Other styles were taken from the East, which was rapidly being opened up by trade and colonization. Many of them wavered uneasily between history and fancy: "Moorish" designs are generally romantically vague, while the existence of an Indian Empire prompted grandiose Kiplingesque fantasies as well as fine work in gold and silver. More authentic vases in Persian styles were made by Minton's, and "Saracenic" tiles made by the greatest 19th-century British potter, William De Morgan, are a particularly striking example of what must be called creative imitation. Lord Leighton, the leading Victorian painter called in De Morgan when he was planning the Arab Hall of his new house in Holland

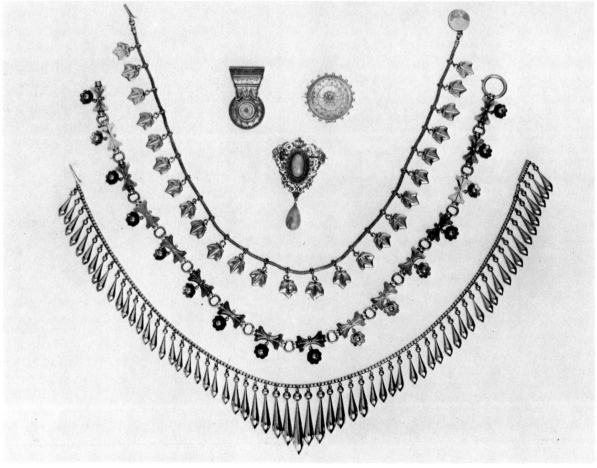

Opposite top *The Arab Hall of Lord Leighton's house. This sumptuous example of Victorian fantasy combines authentic Near Eastern materials with tiles by De Morgan and a frieze by Walter Crane.*

Opposite bottom *Jewelry in the Etruscan style. The Etruscans dominated central Italy before the Romans, but their civilization had only begun to be investigated scientifically in the 19th century.*

Left *These tiles by William De Morgan are also from Leighton House. The blues and greens are typical of De Morgan's "Persian" designs.*

Park Road, London. The hall is a high tiled room with a splendid fountain cut from a single block of black marble, lattice screens, marble columns and a dome. It is a delightfully exotic example of Victorian Moorish; apart from the glittering frieze by Walter Crane, most of the materials are authentically Near Eastern, but the mood and presentation are decidedly Victorian. The tiles are also not quite authentic. Leighton's collection was not large enough for his purposes, and he therefore asked De Morgan to make tiles that would complete and complement the existing designs—which De Morgan did to such effect that the visitor finds it impossible to distinguish between his creations and the originals. It is perhaps not out of place here to mention that Leighton House is open to the public, and that the Arab Hall, the separate displays of De Morgan pottery and the collection of paintings give one an excellent idea of High Victorian taste.

Another impressive technical rediscovery was made by the Roman jeweler Fortunato Pio Castellani. He observed that the ancient Etruscan technique of granulation was still in use among the peasants of Umbria, and persuaded some of them to instruct his own workmen. The technique involved soldering minute grains of gold on to a metal body without unsightly clogging. Amazingly, 19th-century versions never quite equalled the 2000-year-old Etruscan work, but they none the less enjoyed a European vogue from the 1860s to the 1890s. Castellani and his descendants produced a great deal of this "Etruscan filigree style" jewelry for export, but much was also made in England. Like De Morgan's tiles, these pieces show one of the most attractive sides of Victorian revivalism.

Schoolmaster Severity.

Realism, Morality and Sentiment

THERE was a strong undercurrent of escapism in the Victorians' taste for historical scenes and styles. The kind of fantasy implicit in the gentleman's Elizabethan library was even more openly expressed in other media—in blood-and-thunder historical dramas and narrative paintings like *When Did You Last See Your Father?* The other side of the coin was a taste for realism in its most literal sense: the laboriously faithful and detailed reproduction of appearances. Like historicism, this kind of realism involved imitation rather than creation, and we have already suggested that it was a way of playing safe which evaded the task of choosing or creating a style. The fineness of the realistic detail was also looked on as guaranteeing the value of an object; for many customers felt—

feel even now—that something that has taken dozens or hundreds of man-hours to produce must be a genuine work of art. But the Victorian impulse towards realism was too powerful and all-embracing to make this convincing as a total explanation. The same impulse is felt, in the 19th-century novel, which has a documentary quality that was new to literature and would have mystified writers or previous centuries. It can hardly be a coincidence that two of the literary battle-cries of the period were "realism" and "naturalism". Perhaps because they were in the process of conquering nature, the Victorians found an apparently inexhaustible pleasure in reproducing reality.

The potted palm and the stuffed bird in its glass case represent the simplest kind of realism, in which the real thing becomes a possession to be put on display. A more

Left *Schoolmaster Severity. This little group was shown at the Great Exhibition, and must have made a strange contrast with the technological marvels all around it.*

Right *Victoriana—on sale even in 1840! The doll is German in origin and has a composition head and peg wooden body. The stall, crammed with goods for sale, is English.*

sophisticated version of the same activity was to use the electroplating (or, more correctly in this case, electrotyping) process to cover real plants, flowers and insects with silver. The ornaments created in this way could easily pass as masterpieces of the silversmith's art, but once recognized for what they are, they seem a little too suggestive of embalmed corpses to suit most tastes. However, they were enormously popular in the 1840s, when the process was perfected. Electrotype-it-yourself kits were put on the market, and the Prince Consort is said to have set aside a special room in order to make his own experiments.

Feather-work and shell-work were popular home hobbies in which natural materials were used. Ladies made patterns of shells in trays, or grottoes and other constructions. Poor children built grottoes in the street and stood by them begging pennies from passers-by. Real birds' feathers were stuck on to paper to make pictures—usually, though not always, of birds. These can be particularly charming and colorful, but again there is something strange about taking the feathers from the real creature to make a two-dimensional copy of it. Feathers could also be used to make flower-sprays, and of course wax and cotton bouquets of flowers and fruit were a feature of most drawing rooms. Like the expensive parian porcelain statuettes, these imitation flowers were carefully preserved under glass covers. The number of such fragile objects must have added considerably to the agonies of housework, a situation reflected in the Careless Housemaid jokes scattered throughout Victorian periodicals. In this case our sympathies lie with the invariably phlegmatic maid rather than with the distraught middle-class victim.

Left and below *English coach lace shown at the Great Exhibition, a fire screen and a coffee cosy.*

Right *Examples of fashionable snake jewelry together with a coral necklace, brooch with plaited hair, and an etui in the form of a human arm*

Nature as ornament

As all this indicates, the Victorians looked above all to nature as a source of inspiration for realistic ornament. For ladies' work in the home, nature was the most easily available model, especially in its tamed and friendly English form. It seems likely too that all the pretty and ingenious compositions made with scraps of fabric, cut-paper, cardboard, cork, beads, hair and leaves, express a certain nostalgia for the life of the countryside. It is always worth bearing in mind that few families in Victorian cities had left their villages and farms more than a generation or two before.

Nature is most often the theme of the needlework with which so many Victorian women occupied themselves. But the most common home craft of all was Berlin work embroidery, a technique devised in Berlin in the early years of the 19th century. This had the tremendous advantage of requiring no skill on the part of the executant; after all, there must have been thousands of women who were not particularly good with their hands. Berlin work enabled the less-than-ideal housewife to impress her husband and beautify the home by just sewing colored wools on to a squared canvas, following the squared paper

pattern in front of her. A cynic might add that this occupation left both mind and tongue free, so that two women could gossip as much as they pleased while being virtuously productive. Berlin work was used for firescreens, for antimacassars, for cushion and chair covers, and even for rugs. It is one of the most typical products of the age, turned out in such enormous quantities that even today it is easy to find in antique shops and relatively inexpensive.

Patchwork and beadwork were typical but contrasted occupations. Patchwork quilts were severely practical objects which used up all the left-over scraps of fabric in the household – and just for that reason they are one of the very few examples of purely abstract designs in the whole range of Victoriana, very colorful and with a largeness and light-hearted quality too rarely found in more artistic productions. At the opposite extreme are the beads sewn on to bags and purses, which must have required endless patience and close attention. Victorian ladies used tiny needles to create bead patterns – commonly delicate little flowers – on fabrics of all sorts, and bead decoration was so popular that it was produced commercially as well.

Naturalistic decoration is found throughout

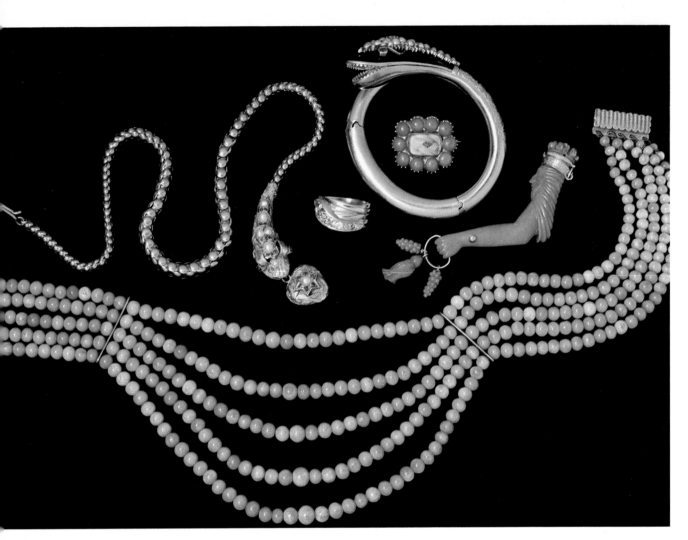

 the entire range of manufactured goods. In many cases it shades off into the historical styles that we have already looked at; the less formalized pieces of Rococo porcelain, for example, could equally well be called naturalistic. The same is true of early and mid-Victorian silver, in which items like centerpieces are covered with a dense mass of leaves, while the handles of knives, forks and spoons are elaborately detailed versions of the kind of food that they were intended to be used for. Palissy ware is obviously an example of extreme naturalism, and most of the other historical styles also include more or less stylized naturalistic decoration.

Mid-Victorian jewelry was very much dominated by naturalism. From the 1850s women wore bulky crinolines, and jewels were correspondingly larger and elaborately set–a trend that was not reversed until the 1870s. Gold or imitation gold settings were usually manufactured in a naturalistic Rococo style. Coral jewelry was all the rage for a time, and was often made up into delicate sprays of berries and flowers. "Scottish" jewelry became fashionable under the influence of Scott's novels and the royal family's enjoyment of Highland holidays at Balmoral.

Ladies wore Cairngorm and grouse-foot brooches, and even the soberly dressed Victorian male sported a cigar case decorated with a ram's head. But perhaps the most typical piece of jewelry was the snake bracelet, which wound round the arm with an often highly convincing realism. A sinister ornament, one would think, for a squeamish lady, but one that outlasted almost all other fashions.

Birds and flowers were innocuous and endearing, and could therefore be used on anything in the home from a jelly mould to a piece of embroidery. The brilliant colors and silky pile of parrots "plush-stitched" on embroidered screens and covers are particularly memorable. On an altogether higher level are the magnificent watercolors by John James Audubon, who traveled across America painting its birds from life. Reproduced as colored aquatints in *Birds of America*, these are rightly recognized as works of art. All sorts of other animals appealed to the Victorians, including beasts made familiar by intrepid travelers and imperial adventurers. Camel and elephant are prominent on a giant antique like the Albert Memorial, which is itself a fascinating compound of Gothic revivalism, imperialist fantasy and naturalism.

Views, events and slogans

Country scenes and landscapes show us another aspect of the taste for nature. On objects such as prints, postcards, embroidery, glass and porcelain, a nostalgic vision of the countryside as a lost paradise is uppermost. Jigsaws and illustrations in children's books give us more naïve versions of the same idea, and so do the colorful transfer-printed lids of pots, on which quaint cottages and farm and village scenes vied in popularity with sporting subjects and royal portraits. Many of the transfers themselves have survived, and people collect them as enthusiastically as they do other kinds of Victoriana. A detail of some interest is that a certain amount of pottery and porcelain was painted with North American scenes and then exported to Canada and the USA— striking evidence of the leading position of the British industry in mid-Victorian times.

The realities of industrialism and town life were less well served, in spite of occasional fashions such as locomotive jewelry. Home was, after all, a refuge from this kind of reality. New machinery, business enterprises, railways, poverty and crime were written about and illustrated in books and periodicals which could be consulted when one chose, but they were not particularly desirable as permanent features of the home environment. Hence, for example, the town views in Victorian prints and paperweights are usually

seaports, rendered with all the emphasis on the picturesque. In terms of atmosphere they are closer to countryside scenes than to any kind of urban realism.

The only objects that really strike the modern note are machines, for the workshop did not exist to be tastefully embellished but to make money. In recent years people have begun to realize that all sorts of fascinating but obsolete installations are disappearing without trace, and "industrial archaeology" has become a respectable academic study. Few of us have room for industrial plant in our houses, but Victorian tools and scientific instruments can still be bought in shops and markets, or even begged from unsuspecting modernizers. There are also sewing machines, phonographs, typewriters and telephones, which represented the latest in personal gadgetry for the middle class. The outsize flower-like attractions of the phonograph are well known, but early typewriters—skeletal objects with the keys rising up in a great bunch— seem to me original "designs" that have not yet been properly appreciated.

The other main contemporary items were those celebrating Victorian progress—and incidentally expressing national pride: the Great Exhibition, for example, and events such as the launching of the *Great Eastern*. The exhibition was celebrated in many media, and there is even a large and peculiarly hideous vase,

Opposite *A cabinet of military relics from London's Army Museum including an Edison phonograph and a Baden-Powell plate.*

Below *Three Staffordshire figures of popular American personalities from the stage and politics.*

made for the exhibition, with medallions of the Queen on one side and of the Crystal Palace on the other. In fact commemorative pieces and souvenirs were Victorian institutions. The silver presentation set, the gold watch for retired employees, earthenware plaques and jugs such as the predominantly black and pink Sunderland ware, engraved glasses, picture postcards, badges—all these were used to record public and personal events. Even political passions found expression, as on the jug lamenting that General Gordon had been betrayed (by the British government), or the teapot proclaiming that against the Boers "though it cost the best of British blood, there is no turning back." But the only events rivaling the Great Exhibition as subjects for commemoration were the Jubilees of 1887 and 1897. For the Diamond Jubilee of 1897 the *Daily Mail* issued *Sixty Years A Queen* in ten sixpenny parts, Mr. Gladstone distributed 1500 Jubilee medals to schoolchildren in his home town of Hawarden, and quantities of Jubilee mugs, dishes, favors and playing cards were given away or sold. Anybody with something to sell tried to cash in by putting a picture of the Queen and a patriotic slogan on wrappers, newspaper advertisements and posters. With time, patience and money it would be possible to build up an impressive collection composed entirely of Jubilee items.

Occasions like these enabled the Victorians to indulge their rather literary and literal artistic taste. The title is an indispensable element in most 19th-century narrative paintings, and titles, mottoes and slogans play an important part in many pieces of Victoriana. The Gordon jug and Boer War teapot have several American equivalents including glass whiskey flasks with such inspiring slogans as "Pike's Peak or Bust". Posters carried elaborate and self-consciously literary messages until late in the century (when designers began to realize that bold outlines and short slogans had greater impact), and advertisements for melodramas such as *Maria Marten (Murder in the Red Barn)* and *The Bells* still make somewhat overstimulating reading. Political cartoons in magazines were even more dependent on apt captions. By contrast with the crowded scenes and grotesque satire of earlier artists such as Rowlandson and Gillray, the drawing in later 19th-century cartoons is simpler and the humor usually more genial. Sir John Tenniel—also famous as the illustrator of the *Alice* books—worked in this vein for *Punch* over a period of fifty years. Much of the pleasure given by the drawings lies in the caricatures of famous personalities, which were funny, generally devoid of malice and instantly recognizable. By the 1890s such caricatures were so popular that large numbers were sold separately as full-length color prints.

Below *Figureheads from the collection in the Cutty Sark. A delightful row of naïve "Eastern" and "Classical" figures, with the Italian liberator Garibaldi at the end.*

Opposite *Staffordshire figures. These form a characteristic selection: Archbishop Cranmer, Sir Robert Peel, Iago and Othello, Victoria and Albert in informal clothes, and a figure of Liberty.*

Portraits and figures

The portrait was one of the greatest of all Victorian passions. The age was one of strenuous individual achievements, and hero-worship was a perfectly acceptable emotion. (Nowadays it tends to be regarded as adolescent, though it flourishes discreetly among all age-groups.) The hero was a cult figure and also an ever-present example, scrutinizing the household from shelf or wall, and silently exhorting its members to be upright and industrious. Victoria and Albert, Mr. Gladstone, Florence Nightingale, General Gordon, Garibaldi, the singer Jenny Lind, Shakespeare and the American evangelists Moody and Sankey appear again and again. And at the very end of the period the Boer War hero Baden-Powell is to be found staring out at us from the surfaces of pots and plates. As always, there were those who took hero-worship to ridiculous extremes, and some people even papered their walls with medallions of Disraeli and other leaders.

Naturally the Queen and Prince Albert were the most popular subjects of all, appearing on everything from posters ("Hudson's Soap–The Subject's Best Friend") to dignified parian busts. The royal family were favorites of George Baxter, who in the middle years of the century produced book illustrations and pictures that could be stuck on tins or boxes or pasted into scrapbooks. Baxter prints were very cheap; their rich, almost painterly colors have made them just as popular with modern collectors, but quite the opposite of cheap. Victoria and Albert were also painted on porcelain plaques set in chair-backs–an idea that seems rather strange, for if you sat back you necessarily squashed one of the royal pair.

Americans shared the taste for portraits and commemorative items, seen in furniture designs such as the Lincoln rocker and the Martha Washington chair. And popular heroes such as Benjamin Franklin and George Washington appear on whiskey flasks as well as on more conventionally dignified objects. A popular novelty for portraits was crystallo-ceramic, a process first patented in 1819 by a

London glassmaker, Apsley Pellat, but only exploited on a large scale in the Victorian period. This consisted of a white-paste figure (called a sulphide) which was embedded in clear glass–with little apparent point except as a demonstration of ingenuity for its own sake. By contrast, carving and painting the wooden figureheads of ships was a traditional art, and the massive simplified forms and bright colors are very refreshing after too long a time spent among smoothly finished Victorian portraits. The collection of figureheads on the old *Cutty Sark*, for example, gives a sort of child's-eye view of Victorian taste, with Greek goddesses, turbaned Moors, figures in contemporary dress, and popular heroes like Abraham Lincoln and Garibaldi.

Many of the cheap Staffordshire pottery figures have the same naïve quality–and many, sad to relate, were the products of child labour. The most common items were "flatbacks", figures or groups intended for the mantelpiece or shelf, with flat unworked backs that could be placed flush against a wall.

They were made for poorer homes and cottages, and give us an interesting insight into a less pretentious taste – the taste, perhaps, of people who bought the kind of standard "mixed" furniture that combined naturalistic carving with vaguely "historical" elements. Portrait figures were usually made in the round, and provide an amazingly extensive record of the period. All the popular heroes are here, and so is almost every contemporary figure of note: the Hungarian revolutionary Kossuth, Napoleon III and his empress, Bismarck and Moltke, the German emperor and his family, Franklin, Washington and Lincoln. There are even figures of the murderers William Palmer and James Rush, a little model of Palmer's house, and a scene of the murder in the red barn – the most curiously macabre of all Victorian mementos.

If proof is needed that talent and not technique is decisive, it is provided by the early history of photography. Despite all the advances of the 20th century, Victorian portrait photography has never been bettered. In France, Carjat and Nadar photographed Baudelaire and George Sand with a sharpness and tonal contrast that gives an effect of intensity and psychological penetration. One of the best British photographers was the gifted amateur Julia Margaret Cameron, who had a knack of coaxing eminent personalities to sit for her. Her photographs have a romantic softness that only occasionally rises to drama, marked in her photographs of children, and in less successful set-pieces such as her illustrations to Tennyson's *Idylls of the King*.

Even earlier photographs of high quality were produced by two Scots, Robert Adamson and David Octavius Hill. They worked with a process that had only just been invented – the calotype, which was the first process to use chemically treated paper instead of unwieldy copper plates, and the first from which more than one print could be taken. Their work suddenly became known to a wide public at the beginning of 1973, when the Royal Academy proposed to put up for auction three albums of photographs compiled by Adamson. A public outcry soon persuaded the Royal Academy to abandon the proposed sale, and the collection is now in the National Portrait Gallery. Being untouched for so long, the photographs were also unfaded, and give us a wonderful picture of early Victorian life – of gentlemen with stovepipe hats, tight-sleeved jackets and untidy, bandage-like cravats, girls with their hair dangling in ringlets, fisherfolk with bare feet or in their finery, and even an elegant Red Indian wearing a frilled shirt under his buckskins.

Moral, religious and educational
Victorian realism was usually tempered by the demands of morality – or, what amounted to much the same thing, respectability. Sexuality was never treated frankly in public; it is notorious that the most puritanical families preferred to call legs – even table legs – limbs, and that they kept both the fleshly and the wooden members covered up. Nature found a banal outlet in prints and postcards which display a rather irritatingly selfconscious naughtiness, and we know that thousands of pornographic books and prints were bought for private perusal. More attractive than either, because straightforward and simple, were the little earthenware objects given as prizes at fairs. These "fairings", with their bedroom scenes ("Mr Jones, remove your hat!") and Married Bliss jokes, are a typical popular mixture of sauciness and sentimentality.

Morality also distorted the Victorians' overall view of reality by insisting that the good must triumph and the wicked go down in defeat. Moral attitudes were reinforced by the all-pervading influence of Christianity. Biblical scenes were popular in all types of illustration including the ubiquitous Berlin embroidery, and religion and royalty are the typical subjects of Baxter prints. Mottoes of the "God Bless This House" type were printed and framed or manufactured in earthenware. The fairing equivalent, "God Bless Our House", has a husband and wife in the middle of a furious row, flinging pillows at each other. Religious subjects appear on Staffordshire figures, where their solemnity is qualified by an air of quaintness. Pope Pius IX, Cardinal Manning and a selection of saints are counterbalanced by the American revivalists Moody and Sankey, and on a more partisan note by Ridley and Latimer at the stake and contrasted figures of Protestantism and Popery. The most touching survivals of Victorian piety are the samplers embroidered as set-pieces by children. The religious verses on them are more than often commonplace, but the labors of a long-dead dutiful child must move even the least sentimental.

Education and edification are recurrent themes in toys (The Picture Alphabet for a Good Child), but Victorian children had more of them, better made and more entertaining, than any children before them: dolls and dolls'

The sea and sermons. The combination on these Sunderland ware plaques must have been found in many Victorian homes.

*The Victorian child was much luckier than his
predecessors. The sturdy, colorful toys here
include pegs and humming tops, American
alphabet blocks, a Scripture cube game, the
Genteel Boy and his Doings, and a clown from an
American toy circus.*

houses, rocking horses, games, picture bricks, mechanical toys, jigsaws, and a whole range of figures and models from Noah's Ark with its animals to coal carts and early cars. Many of them were manufactured in Germany, which had a tradition going back for centuries.

Literature especially for children came into its own during the Victorian period. The only pre-Victorian children's classics are versions of folk-tales and the "story-lines" of adult books such as *Gulliver's Travels* and *Robinson Crusoe*; Victorian writers created books like *The Secret Garden* and *The Railway Children,* so effective that they have been serialized for modern children on television and made into films. Illustrating children's books became a profession needing a special kind of talent. Kate Greenaway, Ralph Caldecott and Walter Crane have become cult figures in recent years, but it is still possible to buy Victorian children's books with colorful and entertaining illustrations by lesser known artists.

Right Victorian dolls. Rosa Mary, Sandy, and the Nurse—easily distinguishable as a member of the lower orders. The kilted boy exemplifies the vogue for things Scottish.

Below The Victorian dream of childhood at its best, sentimental but very appealing. This, appropriately enough, is a nursery screen.

Sentimentalia

With their strong tendency to give reality a moral twist, the Victorians easily slipped into sentimentality. It was they who developed the kind of cloying, over-effusive attitude towards the home, animals, children and the royal family that has never been completely scrubbed out of the Anglo-Saxon soul. All the subjects we have looked at—nature and scenery, remembrances and souvenirs, mottoes, portraits, religion, toys—come together here as vehicles of sentiment. Again we get a wide view of the subject from the little earthenware objects made for the mantelpiece. Pastille burners to sweeten the air of the home were often made in the form of quaint miniature cottages and castles surrounded by "shredded clay" vegeta-

tion. (Later in the century, as hygiene improved, these burners became less common.) There were sentimental scenes with captions (The Soldier's Dream, Highland Jamie) and quantities of shaggy little dogs; one of the consequences of urbanization was that dogs figured less and less in people's lives as hunting companions, and more and more as pets to be looked after and loved. But Victorian attitudes towards animals were just as contradictory as ours. Sir Edwin Landseer made a fortune by painting pictures like *The Monarch of the Glen* and *Dignity and Impudence,* bought by thousands of people as engravings. On the other hand hunting scenes remained as popular as ever, and squeamish ladies adorned themselves with furs and ostrich feathers. The contradiction,

Left *Fairings. These china objects were given as prizes at fairs. The mixture of sentiment and broad humor is very refreshing.*

Below *Jet jewelry for mourning.*

which has persisted ever since, is probably a product of town life, in which the realities of both the slaughterhouse and the hunting field are equally remote.

But sentimentality was not just an incomprehensible abberation on the part of the Victorians. Like the cult of the home, it was a protective reaction against the surrounding darkness and violence. And it was also a way of coping with the personal tragedies that were an everyday part of 19th-century life. Deaths, particularly the deaths of children, occurred frequently and inside the home itself. When Dickens and his readers wept over the death of Little Nell they were finding an outlet for feelings that it would perhaps not have been manly to express fully in the real situation.

Mourning was certainly common enough to support a separate trade in jewelry as well as in dress. Jet jewelry, much sought-after in the last few years, was made primarily for mourning, and its production helped the town of Whitby to flourish. Jet is impressively plain and smooth, but also attractive–for the lady who spent years in full or half mourning could hardly be expected to indulge in the dowdiness of grief. Bracelets made from the hair of a loved-one (living or dead) have always seemed too personal for preservation or collection, and almost all of them have vanished. Some were converted into jewelry by being intertwined with gold, and patterns and pictures made out of hair were set into brooches. Lockets and pendants with compartments for locks of hair had a much longer-lasting popularity. Miniatures of loved-ones were set into lockets or brooches, or worn on gentlemen's watch-chains. And a lady with a large family might string together miniatures of the members to make a bracelet.

At the opposite extreme from the gravity of mourning was Christmas, which could almost be called a Victorian invention. Its apotheosis–

Opposite *Mourning jewelry. Hair and gold jewelry: a chain and cross, and earrings. The verses on the card, addressed by the deceased to his wife and children, are a macabre touch.*

Below *The Victorians celebrated as ostentatiously as they mourned. The music-hall programs, Valentines and Christmas cards all display a rather self-conscious gaiety.*

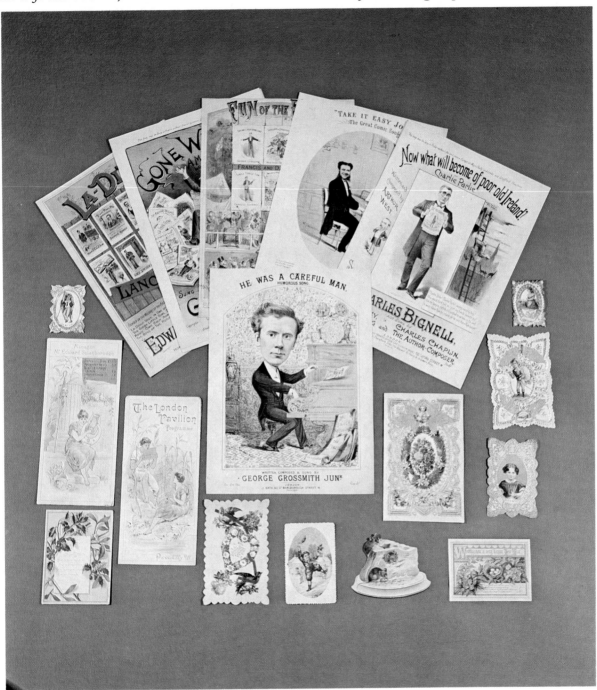

presents all round and everybody over-eating in front of a blazing fire—is part of our mental picture of the age. The commercialization of Christmas, still lamented every December, began at least a hundred years ago in Victorian times. The Christmas card first became big business in the 1870s, and though styles have changed there is scarcely any technique or device on modern cards that was not exploited by our ancestors. There were gilded cards, frosted cards, paper-lace cards, cards dusted with bronze, and cards with multiple layers and embossed silver or gold paper. Some trick cards carried cut-out fronts that framed or half-concealed subjects on the following sheet; others contained comic or sentimental figures with movable arms and legs. New Year's cards, greetings cards, Valentines and calendars display the same sort of ingenuity and were equally commercialized. A few greetings cards even anticipate the 1960s in being jokingly uncomplimentary, and satire and even politics occur from time to time. Many cards were designed by well-known artists. The best are undoubtedly by Kate Greenaway, the illustrator of children's books.

Personal mementos played a great part in social life, and ranged from humble "Remember Me" jugs to corbeilles (pre-wedding gifts of jewelry, given by the upper-class bridegroom to his intended). Let us end this chapter with a look at a special object of British sentiment: sailors and the sea. Sailors were traditionally supposed to while away the long days at sea by making keepsakes for their sweethearts. This was true as far as it went, though the results were usually unsophisticated; even most of the ships in bottles seem to have been made by landlubbers. But popular belief attributed to sailors many objects that were in fact manufactured. When and where they could have spun and blown glass is a mystery,

but they were all the same supposed to have made some of the glass novelties called "friggers" – walking sticks, pipes, and of course ships. A more plausible but equally fallacious attribution was the "sailor's Valentine". This was a hinged wooden box that opened out flat to reveal a pattern of shells, usually with a heart and a loving message. Sailors' Valentines are charming, naïvely nautical objects; but they were made for exports in Barbados.

For us, all these models and pictures and messages are a fascinating glimpse of the past. For intelligent Victorians, surrounded by them, they seemed both stifling and trivial. Their attempts to create something better are the subject of the next section.

50

Artists, Craftsmen and Aesthetes

WE have seen that historical styles multiplied in the 1830s, and that the objects manufactured were growing heavier and steadily more elaborate. Even at this early date there were designers and critics who were worried by the situation, for the Victorians were nothing if not design-conscious. The School of Design was founded in 1837, and several magazines dealing with the subject were set up in the next few years. The Prince Consort took an active interest in it, and the Great Exhibition was intended as a stimulus to better design as well as a display of British skills. A direct attempt to reform design was made by Henry Cole, later head of the Victoria and Albert Museum. Under the pseudonym Felix Summerly, Cole set up Summerly's Art Manufactures, which employed painters and sculptors such as Alfred Stevens to provide designs for manufacturers. The purpose was a noble one, but the solution was based on a misconception–that a piece of furniture or a stove was a sort of mini-sculpture which could be created by a fine artist without any of the specialized knowledge possessed by the humble applied artist/craftsman at his workbench. Neither Cole nor his artists realized that every material had to be treated according to its special qualities and with close consideration of the function to be performed by the final product. The result was a mass of work with an imposing air and dense naturalistic ornament–work that looks to us as Victorian as anything else produced during the period.

Opposite *Shellwork, like other crafts that lent themselves to very elaborate work, was popular as both a home hobby and a commercial product.*

Left *Design for a stove in Renaissance style, by Alfred Stevens, very much a miniature palace.*

Opposite *"Strawberry Thief" wallpaper by William Morris. Morris's colorful symmetrical designs have become very popular again in recent years.*

Below *The "St George" cabinet is attractively "primitive" in appearance. It was designed by Philip Webb and painted by William Morris with scenes from the life of St George.*

William Morris and "the Firm"

Pugin's work, with its emphasis on honest craftsmanship, pointed a better way forward. His message was taken up by the great Victorian pundit John Ruskin, whose books treated art as a matter of serious moral decision, and was put into practice by William Morris. Morris was a man of the diverse attainments: he was a poet, a painter, a designer, a medievalist and a socialist. He loathed the mechanized tastelessness of Victorian products, and at the time of the Great Exhibition simply refused to look around. But his active involvement with design began after he commissioned Philip Webb to build him a house—the Red House at Bexleyheath, which was itself a revolutionary design because of its simple red brick construction and functional efficiency.

When Morris came to furnish the Red House, he found that there was nothing on the market the he could tolerate inside his home. Typically, he decided that the only answer was to go into the business himself. In 1861 he and a group of friends founded Morris, Marshall, Faulkner and Company—soon known affectionately to the avant-garde as "the Firm"—in Red Lion Square, London. The Firm made fabrics, furniture, glass and other domestic goods. Morris's own talent was for flat, two-dimensional designs—textiles, wallpaper and stained glass. His wallpaper, with its dense patterned flowers and foliage, has been revived with great success in recent years. He painted furniture too, but did not design it. None the less, although Webb and the painters Rossetti and Burne-Jones were intermittently

involved with the Firm, it was undoubtedly Morris who provided its inspiration and drive – and also its capital. Morris & Co. began to attract public attention in 1862, when they took part in the international exhibition of that year; and their participation made it in many ways a more significant event in design history than the Great Exhibition eleven years before.

The style of Morris & Co. was not incomprehensible to the public, for it was the Gothic style which had been in use for some thirty years. Morris was a wholehearted medievalist. As a painter he was a follower of the Pre-Raphaelites, influenced mainly by the dreamy atmosphere of courtly love in the paintings of Rossetti. But like Ruskin he also saw the Middle Ages as a time when the craftsman took pleasure in the work of his hands – when what he did was meaningful work and not mere mindless repetitive labor as in the 19th-century factory. (Morris's dislike of poverty and vulgarity later led to his conversion to socialism. His finest prose works, *A Dream of John Ball* and *News from Nowhere,* are visions of a sort of transformed Middle Ages brought about by the Socialist Revolution.) These convictions meant that Morris Gothic was Gothic with a difference. A piece like the St George cabinet, designed for the Firm by Philip Webb, is plainer than popular Gothic, and all the joints are revealed, giving it an attractively rugged look. Instead of elaborate carving there are panels painted by Morris. And the inspiration of the design is not pinnacled late Gothic but the ruder, weightier style of the 13th century.

The trouble about furniture designed by one master and painted by another was that it cost a good deal to buy; and the same was true of Morris's beautiful hand-woven fabrics and almost all of his work except his wallpaper. Morris's distrust of machinery created a contradiction in his program. He sought to revive craftsmanship and at the same time to bring artistically made goods to the people – a thing that was only possible if the goods were produced cheaply by machine production. For this reason only the Firm's chairs reached a really wide public. One of these was the Sussex chair, a green-stained rush-seated form adapted directly from country types that were still being produced. The popularity of the Morris & Co. versions, many of them designed by Ford Madox Brown, led to the promotion of the type from the kitchen to the drawing room. Even more widely popular was the so-called Morris chair, an upholstered version

of the Sussex chair with bobbin-turned decoration and an adjustable back. This was made from about 1866 and established itself very firmly in America, where it remained fashionable right down to the end of the century.

Part of Morris's doctrine was "truth to materials", which he regarded as a pre-eminently medieval virtue. Basically this meant that you should not torture naturally inflexible materials into fluid, intricate shapes, or make rigid structures out of naturally pliable materials. This may appear straightforward and sensible enough now, but it contradicted the Victorian assumption that good craftsmanship largely consisted in overcoming the resistance of matter. Ruskin had championed Morris's view some years before. "The peculiar qualities of glass are ductility when heated and transparency when cold . . . All work is bad which does not with loud voice proclaim one or other of these qualities. Consequently all cut glass is barbarous." Cut glass was already going out of fashion when Ruskin wrote these lines in *The Stones of Venice,* but his influence was largely responsible for the popularity of "Venetian" glass in the mid-Victorian period. The set of glasses designed by Philip Webb in 1859 represent a more genuine response to the Ruskin-Morris doctrine. These glasses are simple and sturdy-looking, with discreet shaping that brings out the "peculiar quality" of ductility on which Ruskin insisted. They were made for William Morris by James Powell and Sons, who were soon the last British firm that still sold hand-made glass; one of the family was Henry Powell, who developed from the Morris tradition to become the most outstanding British exponent of Art Nouveau glassmaking.

The potter William De Morgan was closely associated with William Morris, though he always worked independently. He was easily the greatest of the art potters inspired by Morris, though he was not quite an artist potter in the modern sense of the word: he was intimately involved with the process of production as designer and supervisor, but left the actual business of throwing the pots to assistants. We have already looked at his impressive work as a designer of tiles (which also included commissions for P & O liners and the Czar's yacht); but his luster-decorated plates, bowls and vases are even more famous. De Morgan rediscovered how to make the luster pigments which gave Near Eastern and Hispano-Moresque pottery their distinctive golden sheen. He was also strongly influenced by Near Eastern and Persian designs, which he applied to simple, very elegant shapes. The results are a superb blend of color, decoration and shape, and many readers may well think that there is nothing else in this book to match the beauty of De Morgan's works. Unfortunately the cost of producing his work was too often greater than the payment De Morgan received for it, and he was usually in financial difficulties. He retired to Italy and gradually designed less and less. Ironically, in old age he became the best-selling author of novels that have since been completely forgotten, and he died during the First World War—of trench fever contracted from a young soldier who insisted on visiting the famous writer.

As well as De Morgan, there were a number of artist potters who carried out all the manufacturing processes by themselves; in a sense they were the ancestors of 20th-century masters like Bernard Leach. Only the Martins have much reputation today, but the movement as a whole did have an effect on commercial manufacturers. In particular, the making of stoneware was revived in the 1870s; for most of the century it had been used only for kitchenware or for jugs in which to keep things hot. The Martins made stoneware, and the exhibition of salt-glazed stoneware by a big firm, Doulton's of Lambeth, showed that at least one section of the public was tiring of smoothly finished pottery and was willing to buy wares in which the nature of the material was more apparent. Doulton's was particularly forward-looking in establishing a link with the Lambeth School of Art, which became a nursery for the firm's future designers. But despite its attractive roughness, it cannot be said that Doulton stoneware, with its rather dingy colors and incised decoration, is very inspiring. Its vogue is of interest to us because it was a sign that things were changing.

Salt-glaze Doulton Stoneware by Hannah Barlow.

55

Below *Doulton stoneware has an attractive roughness of texture that is rare in 19th-century pottery.*

Bottom *Lusterware by William De Morgan, with magnificent designs that are skilfully fitted into the shape of dishes and vases.*

Below *Doulton stoneware has an attractive roughness of texture that is rare in 19th-century pottery.*

Bottom *Lusterware by William De Morgan, with magnificent designs that are skilfully fitted into the shape of dishes and vases.*

*Cupboard and secretaire designed by William
Burges. Burges was an uncompromising exponent
of the Gothic Style.*

Progressive design and "art furniture"

This was also true of furniture. Morris & Co.'s original designs may not have been bought by a wide public, but their example was followed by a number of important designers. Among them were architects like William Burges and Richard Norman Shaw, whose cabinets, sideboards and bookcases were even larger and more rudely massive than the Morris pieces. Burges in particular was a propagandist of the early Gothic style, making much use of paint, gilding and inset materials. His work has aroused a good deal of interest in recent years, though to some tastes his pieces are over-large and awkward-looking.

Unlike Shaw and Burges, Bruce Talbot was a full-time furniture designer with a national reputation. Like them, he made massive Early English furniture. And like Morris & Co., he made a point of not concealing its construction – in fact Talbert's large Gothic strap hinges are an ostentatious kind of personal signature. For decorating sideboards – his most character-istic pieces – he preferred shallow carving and inlaid low-relief metal panels to the painting favored by other designers.

Talbert was a powerful influence on the art furniture that many people began buying in the 1870s. This was a commercial version of progressive Gothic, often combined with features influenced by Japanese art. Lightly constructed pieces of ebonized wood replaced oak and mahogany, straight lines and angles replaced curves, and carving gave way to

Opposite *This interior from Cardiff Castle was designed by Burges, and shows the amazing extremes to which Gothic could be taken.*

Left *American Eastlake furniture, made by the Herter brothers around 1882. Though lavishly decorated, it has a simple rectangular shape.*

painted panels and simple turned members. Indirectly the use of surface decoration on art furniture must also have given an impetus to the revival of 18th-century styles in which inlays and brighter woods were employed. The importance of art furniture has probably been underestimated, though it must be admitted that many pieces are not really more than debased or misunderstood versions of progressive designs, foisted upon a gullible public that was set upon following avant-garde fashion rather than developing a genuine taste of its own.

One of the most influential writers on design was Charles Lock Eastlake, whose *Hints on Household Taste* (1868) went into several editions, championing a cheap, almost un-

decorated form of Gothic. Its greatest impact was in the USA, where the *Hints* were published in 1870. "Eastlake furniture" became a recognized type, sturdy and practical, with framed paneling and false drawer fronts. Though historical styles and generous upholstering were as characteristic of American as of British furniture, regional and immigrant styles helped to sustain a stronger tradition of plainness than in Britain.

In however distorted a form, art furniture reached a wide public, though many people still opted for more conservative historical styles. From the 1870s the avant-garde trend was reinforced by new influences, and contemporaries became aware of a new movement which they labelled "Aesthetic".

The Aesthetic Movement

The public image of an aesthete was a languid young man holding a lily or sunflower, or an intense young woman with flowing Pre-Raphaelite hair, a long dress and a string of amber beads round her neck. Cartoonists like George Du Maurier of *Punch* made great play with these extraordinary creatures and their very exaggerated devotion to art, and the philistine attitude of mixed contempt and fascination has interesting parallels in the reaction to the Bloomsbury Group of the 1900s and the beatniks and hippies of the 1960s.

Two public personalities were popularly identified with aestheticism: the young Oscar Wilde (poet and journalist but not yet an important playwright) and the American painter James McNeil Whistler. Both were fond of giving lectures, and both supported the heretical doctrine of "art for art's sake", which was particularly shocking to a generation brought up to believe that art had a moral purpose. To compound the offence, both were notable wits–and though humor and even satire were enjoyed with gusto by the Victorians, the acidity and detachment of wit was incompatible with the kind of committed earnestness they admired. Wilde's affected languor became the butt of cartoonists and reviewers, and the public was entertained by the pugnacious Whistler's lawsuit against Ruskin, who had made insulting remarks about the painter's *Nocturnes*. Ruskin's conviction that Whistler was "flinging a pot of paint in the public's face" provides an interesting if not uncommon example of the rebel of one generation being outraged by the still more radical attitudes of the next.

As usual, the public idea of what was happening was not very accurate, and the antics of public personalities only obscured the issues. As everybody knew, people who could be recognized at sight as aesthetes were part of a tiny minority; and furthermore there was no organized Aesthetic Movement and no Aesthetic Manifesto. But something *was* happening all the same; and that was a shift in taste affecting quite a large section of the public–including many of the people who laughed at the *Punch* jokes. Perhaps the shakier prosperity of the 1870s and the emergence of foreign competitors was responsible for the change from the mid-Victorian mood. Perhaps there was simply the usual reaction against the taste of the previous generation. Whatever the reason, many people now began to value the artistic and tasteful above stuffy comfort and solidity, and many of them craved for a new elegance and color in their surroundings.

The vogue of art furniture, which became sufficiently established to rate as a recognized trade term, was an important element in the Aesthetic Movement. Medievalism remained strong, and in Gilbert and Sullivan's *Patience* the archetypal aesthete, modeled on Oscar Wilde, "walks down the Strand with a medieval lily in his medieval hand". *The Mikado* is equally pertinent in taking off the great fashion for things Japanese, though it was a belated effort, parodying in 1885 a phenomenon that first became marked in the 1870s.

Japan had been open to the West only since the 1850s, and the qualities of Japanese art–its unique combination of delicacy, boldness of line and bright pure color–came as a revelation. Japanese color prints strongly influenced Toulouse-Lautrec and other French artists, but in Britain it was the book illustrators who responded rather than the painters (with the exception of Whistler). The peacock, standing for all that was gorgeous and extravagant in Japanese and Near Eastern art, was taken up by artists and aesthetes alike. Whistler used it as a signature on his paintings, Crane put peacocks

Opposite *Delicate fan made from paper mâché and decorated in the Japanese style.*

Below *The peacock was the chief symbol of 19th-century aestheticism. Here it appears on Walter Crane's frieze for the Arab Hall in Leighton House.*

Bottom *E. W. Godwin's famous sideboard in "Japanese" style, made by William Wyatt around 1867. It is a spare, very original creation that might well have been produced by a contemporary designer.*

into his lovely "Persian" mosaic frieze for Leighton's Arab Hall, and the gaudy bird appeared in many other interior designs as a symbol of beauty unadulterated by "meaning", outdistancing even the sunflower as a hallmark of aestheticism. Out-and-out aesthetes placed Japanese fans on their walls, put up Japanese screens, and bought Japanese-type furniture for the drawing room.

One of the first designers to exploit this rich new source of motifs was the architect and interior designer E. W. Godwin. (Godwin worked in the Gothic style as well as in the Japanese, and also in the Queen Anne style introduced into architecture in the 1870s—an interesting illustration of the connections between the various progressive tendencies.) As early as 1867, Godwin designed a sideboard inspired by Japanese furniture that still looks stunningly original today. There is one made to the same design in the Victoria and Albert Museum, with gleaming ebonized wood and silver-plated fittings. It has all the spareness of Japanese design, and the pattern of straight vertical and horizontal lines is in the greatest possible contrast to the opulence of mid-Victorian furniture.

Below *"Clutha" glass by Christopher Dresser,
one of the most original of late-Victorian
designers.*

Opposite page *Furniture by Macmurdo. It is
generally plain, but the fretted chair back and the
design on the screen have a flame-like pattern that
anticipates Art Nouveau.*

Unfortunately, as so often in the Victorian period, designs like Godwin's were imitated and debased by enterprising but tasteless manufacturers. While Japanese-style designs, however fanciful, were often acceptable in jewelry, porcelain and other goods, they required particular discretion in furniture, which had different functions in East and West. Since the discretion was lacking, there was a spate of pieces on which superficially Japanese decoration was applied to European forms, frequently with disastrous effects.

The Japanese cult gave rise to a fashion for Oriental art and exotica of all kinds. Poets and painters competed furiously to acquire Chinese blue and white porcelain, and stores began to open departments with a selection of Oriental goods for sale. Still more of these became available when Arthur Lasenby Liberty opened his famous store in Regent Street in 1875. Liberty's sold mainly Oriental goods – lacquered and bamboo furniture, fabrics, carpets, porcelain, bronzes, screens, fans and curios – to a band of Western admirers that included William Morris, the Rossettis and even Thomas Carlyle. In the next few years the firm was to play a role of great importance in disseminating new ideas in design.

One of the few designers of the period who actually visited Japan was Christopher Dresser, who acted as a buyer for his own and other firms. All Dresser's work shows a taste for simple forms and broad decorative effects that was unusual even in the adventurous 1870s and 1880s. He designed pottery and streaked and bubbled "Clutha" glass, but his most effective work was in silver. This was influenced by the economy of Japanese design, but it has a functional elegance that is original and strongly reminiscent of the Art Deco work of fifty years later. Dresser was more modern-minded than Morris and his followers, and showed no reluctance to design for machine production. Many of his designs were translated into electroplate or imitated by other manufacturers, so they are still quite common.

The Arts and Crafts Movement
As a design reformer and the effective originator of art furniture, William Morris can be regarded as one of the founders of the Aesthetic Movement. In the 1880s, at the height of the movement, his advocacy of the medieval craft system influenced some artists and designers to take a rather different direction – to set up guilds and societies in imitation of medieval associations, and to try and revitalize English craftsmanship.

The first event in this, the Arts and Crafts Movement, was the foundation of the Century Guild in 1882. Its central figure was the architect A. H. Mackmurdo, who as one of the editors of the guild's magazine, *Hobby Horse*, helped to make book design a matter of serious artistic concern. Contacts between designers and craftsmen were further promoted by the foundation of St George's Art Society in 1883 and the Art Workers' Guild in 1884. The movement culminated in the establishment of the Arts and Crafts Exhibiting Society in 1888, which brought together all those who shared Morris's principles. The society's first exhibition took place in the same year, and further exhibitions were held at regular intervals down to the end of the century.

The unity of the movement was only superficial, however. Its members believed in co-operative craft principles, and in abolishing the distinction between fine and applied art; but there was no common Arts and Crafts style. In furniture, rural models, Morris Gothic and a discreet Renaissance were most usual, but in other media designers adopted or adapted a variety of past styles, though they were

mainly drawn to rougher, more textured models than their counterparts among conventional revivalists. Morris himself, when he took up weaving, modeled his work on Italian Renaissance designs, and C. R. Ashbee's Renaissance-style jewelry has already been noticed. Ashbee was one of the most influential figures in the Arts and Crafts Movement, founding his own School of Handicraft in 1888. He designed furniture too, but his silver is more distinctive, eventually approaching the Art Nouveau style that was to dominate the 1890s. This tendency is even more noticeable in Arts and Crafts fabrics and wallpaper, where plant decorations were taking on an increasingly sinuous, flame-like quality.

Like the products of Morris & Co., most of these works were expensive, and so only reached an upper-middle-class clientele. But popular taste was slowly evolving, and trade designs absorbed Arts and Crafts ideas just as they had absorbed Morris medievalism and *japonaiserie*. The Arts and Crafts Movement itself was strongly imbued with Morris's anti-machine ideology, though its members tended to protest that this was a misunderstanding of their intentions. The revival of art needlework–in itself an admirable achievement–indicates the ethos of Arts and Crafts, which was closer in spirit to the sandaled "simple-lifer" like the poet Edward Carpenter than to modern machine production.

Above *Gothic-style sideboard of striking simplicity by Philip Webb.*

Right *Silver and gold pendant set with pearls by C. R. Ashbee.*

APPLICATIONS OF ARRASENE FOR DECORATIVE EMBROIDERY

SUPPLIED BY THE BRADFORD ART NEEDLEWORK SOCIETY

1.—DRAPED CHAIR BACK.

2.—DECORATED FAN.

4.—BOOK COVER OR BLOTTING CASE.

3.—DECORATED BELLOWS.

5.—CUSHION.

6.—CUSHION.

The "back to nature" side of the movement emerges most clearly in the Cotswold School. This had its origin in the furniture-making business of Kenton & Co., set up by Ernest Gimson, the brothers Sidney and Ernest Barnsley, and W. R. Lethaby. All three were architects, like Shaw, Burges and Godwin a few years earlier, and we shall come across several more architects who contributed to the development of late-19th-century furniture and interior design. When Kenton and Co. failed in 1892, Lethaby remained in London as head of the new Central School of Arts and Crafts, becoming one of the most prominent figures in the movement. Gimson and the Barnsleys abandoned urban and industrial England for the Cotswolds, where they began to produce furniture in the old cottage tradition of Morris & Co.; ironically, Morris's firm was now mainly producing rather more elaborate furniture with marquetry decoration. The Cotswold School turned out solid, practical furniture made of oak and often modestly decorated with inlays. Gimson was the most talented of the three designers, but unlike the Barnsleys he did not make his own furniture; their collaboration as a group epitomized the Arts and Crafts ideal of integrated design and craftsmanship. It also performed the invaluable service of carrying the neglected vernacular tradition of Morris furniture into the early years of the 20th century, when it became part of the modern revolution in design.

Morris himself remained active in the Arts and Crafts Movement until his death in 1896, though his influence had long ceased to be particularly revolutionary. He made another decisive contribution to design in 1891, when he founded the Kelmscott Press. This was the first of a number of private presses that were to revolutionize typography. Through them, clean, well-designed print became the norm, and the page came to be seen as a unified design embracing print, spacing, margins and illustrations. Morris designed several types, the best-known being the "Chaucer" for the Kelmscott edition of the poet's works, which is generally recognized as the firm's masterpiece. Morris's commitment to socialism led him into contact with the Social Democratic Federation and the new and more hard-headed Fabian Society. The importance of his prestige is reflected in many an old socialist tract, in which there is a juxtaposition of Marxian economics and patterned floral headings and covers that now seems strangely incongruous.

By the 1890s a new and radical art movement had emerged. Art Nouveau, prepared by the Aesthetic Movement and overlapping at many points with Arts and Crafts, ended the period in a spirit and style that amazed and outraged survivors of the early Victorian age.

Opposite *Oak sideboard, carved and inlaid with ebony, sycamore and bleached mahogany. It was designed by W. R. Lethaby.*

Below *Late 19th-century designers had a strong taste for elongated forms. This ladderback chair by Ernest Gimson is a characteristic piece.*

Art Nouveau

A RT Nouveau was the first and only
original style created in the Victorian
period. Here, revival styles, tags and anecdotal
scenes are left far behind, and we are plunged
into a world of long, sinuous lines and elegant,
extravagant figures. The main characteristic of
the new style was the use of real or suggested
plant forms, sinuous or writhing and usually
elongated. Their vigorous living lines, applied
to other shapes and subjects, gave Art Nouveau
its famous "whiplash" look. It was a decisive
and fully conscious break with the past, and
ultimately led on to the abstract and functional
character of modern design. Art Nouveau and
the Modern Movement became involved in a
complicated relationship of mutual influence
and antagonism, and elements of both are
often present in the work of individual artists.

Art Nouveau was an international phenomenon that occurred all over Europe from
London to Vienna. When most people hear the
name now, they probably think first of such
Continental figures as the poster artist Alphonse
Mucha, the Belgian architect Victor Horta, or
Hector Guimard, who created the wrought-
iron entrances to the Paris Métro, with their
gracefully drooping flowers. Yet in fact
the earliest manifestations of Art Nouveau
were British. In the 1880s, for example, William
Morris's wallpaper designs were growing more
intricate and elongated, and in the works of
the illustrators–especially Walter Crane–a
weaving, tendril-like quality became marked in
the drawing of flowers and trees. The Arts and
Crafts Movement, with its rejection of the
distinction between fine and applied art, was
sympathetic to Art Nouveau designers abroad,
and designs by Morris, Crane, Ashbee and
Caldecott were exhibited (especially in
Brussels) early in the 1890s. Poster artists,
interior designers and even painters acknow-
ledged the influence of the British school at a
time when the public at home was at best
only half-aware that anything had happened.

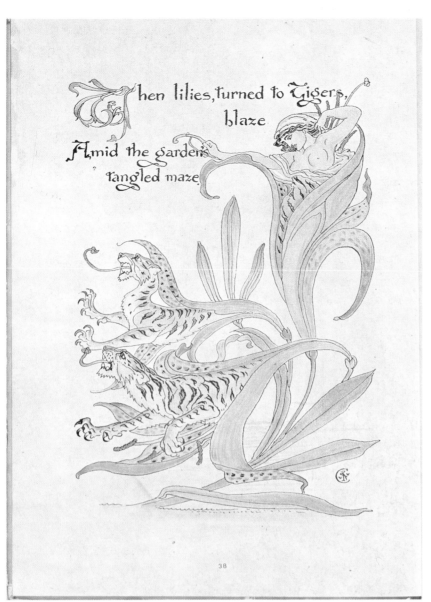

When lilies, turned to Tigers, blaze

Amid the garden's tangled maze

38

Opposite page *Group of typical Art Nouveau objects: a mirror, a picture frame and an ashtray.*

Left *The tendril-like forms of Art Nouveau first appeared in the 1880s. One of the pioneers was Walter Crane, whose illustrations for children's books had a considerable influence on Continental art.*

Below *The Peacock sconce, made of steel, bronze, brass and silver, and designed by Alex Fisher. It was first shown at the Arts and Crafts Exhibition of 1899.*

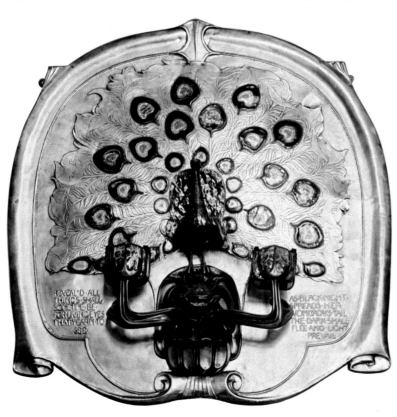

REVEAL'D ALL THINGS SHALL SOME TIME BE FOR LIVING EYES THAT CARE TO SEE

AS BLACK NIGHT SPREADS HER WONDROUS TAIL THE DARK SHALL FLEE AND LIGHT PREVAIL

Mackmurdo, Voysey and Mackintosh

The British artists who had the greatest influence of all on the Continent were A. H. Mackmurdo, C. F. A. Voysey and Charles Rennie Mackintosh; again it is a notable fact that all three were architects. Mackmurdo was the earliest, and as founder of the Century Guild could be called the initiator of the whole Arts and Crafts Movement. His book *Wren's City Churches,* published in 1883, has a title-page with swirling tendrils and elongated birds that goes far beyond anything found in the Morris tradition, and it has understandably been called the first Art Nouveau design. A possible rival is a chair that Mackmurdo designed shortly before, which has a similarly flame-like pattern cut into its back. His designs for cretonnes and wallpapers are even more overtly Art Nouveau, and his furniture, though generally restrained and rectilinear in structure, has a distinctive elongated quality, flame-like fretwork decoration and silk panelling (as on the well-known screen of 1884), and other mannerisms that were to become typical of the new style.

Voysey was an even more important figure. From about 1890 until the First World War he was the leading British architect of country

Opposite *Furniture by Voysey in a late Victorian interior. The craftsmanlike simplicity of his pieces is striking.*

Below *The Mackintosh room in the Glasgow School of Art—a superb pattern of elongated light and dark forms.*

houses, which he designed as comfortable, unpretentious homes that fitted easily into their natural surroundings. Like most progressive architects of the period he designed all the interior decoration of his houses and furnishings, but even in the 1880s, under Mackmurdo's influence, he was designing textiles and furniture that gave him an important place in the history of Art Nouveau.

A certain restraint and regard for fitness of purpose appears in all Voysey's designs and limit their affinities with Art Nouveau. In fact British Art Nouveau, as practised by the leading designers, never became as ornate and exotic as Art Nouveau on the Continent. The whole Arts and Crafts tradition favored relatively simple forms and quiet decoration, and the very fact that British design had been advancing steadily since the 1860s made for a less excitable reaction to the evolution of Art Nouveau. This led to a paradoxical situation: British designers were widely admired abroad, and Voysey's furniture was exported in quantity to France and Belgium; but when Continental Art Nouveau became known in Britain it was publicly denounced by Voysey, Crane and most of the other artists who had done so much to create it.

Below *Voysey wallpaper, with stylized pattern of birds, leaves and flowers.*

Bottom *The title page of Mackmurdo's* Wren's City Churches.

The Art Nouveau element in Voysey's work is most apparent in his textile designs, in which snakes slide round curling ferns in repeated patterns, and elongated bell-shaped flowers rise from a heaving sea-like earth on impossibly long stems. This too was typical of advanced English designers. From Morris and Crane through to Aubrey Beardsley, they produced their most densely decorative work on flat, two-dimensional surfaces that lent themselves to firmly outlined patterning. And we shall find that the most unmistakably Art Nouveau media in Britain were fabrics, wallpaper, graphic art and book design.

Voysey's furniture is even simpler than most Arts and Crafts work – executed in unvarnished oak and with almost no decoration other than its metal hinges. It is strongly reminiscent of Mackmurdo's in its stress on verticals and employment of flat-capped members rising up from the body along the line of the legs. The vertical stress in British Art Nouveau furniture often makes it look odd when viewed in isolation; to be properly appreciated it

Charles Rennie Mackintosh was one of the most original figures in 19th-century British art. This cabinet shows the two main elements in his style:

long, austere forms combined with decadent-looking decoration in the shape of a sinister woman with a "rose-ball".

should be seen in the interiors for which it was designed. The most striking pieces from this point of view are the chairs with their long, straight or slightly sloping backs. The ladder-back chair was particularly popular, the rungs on its back lending themselves to an effective contrast of short horizontals and long verticals.

In the furniture designed by Mackintosh, elongation became a pronounced mannerism: some of his chair backs are as much as five feet high. Mackintosh was a rather isolated figure. Most of his work was done in Glasgow, where he built the School of Art, and he never had much contact with the Arts and Crafts Movement or achieved much recognition in England. On the Continent, however, and especially in Vienna, he had a considerable reputation. Despite the mannerisms of his style, it integrated Art Nouveau curves in an original way, with the kind of clearly defined structure found in the works of Voysey and Mackmurdo—the common element that made all three men precursors of the Modern Movement. Mackintosh too, designed all the

furnishings of his buildings, and his ironwork for the Glasgow School of Art is the best British example of a design in this malleable metal, which was particularly well suited to the flowing Art Nouveau line. Mackintosh and his friend Herbert McNair worked with and eventually married the Macdonald sisters, Frances and Margaret, and the group (called the Four, or, more cavalierly, "the four Macs") developed their own version of Art Nouveau decoration with tightly closed "rose-balls" or flower buds on the ends of elongated stalks. Mackintosh's best work employs these motifs very sparingly—most originally in his metal-work, where they become more or less abstract, and perhaps most effectively on a piece of furniture like his enameled wood cabinet of 1902, on each door of which a stylized, elongated woman kisses a rose-ball.

Mackmurdo, Voysey and Mackintosh represent the most highly conscious and progressive side of Art Nouveau, and just for this reason are not entirely typical. Commercial Art Nouveau was much closer in spirit to the

Chair designed and produced by the famous firm of Liberty.

Opposite *A typically erotic and sinister illustration for* Salome *by Aubrey Beardsley.*

Continental movement. When we compare this popular Art Nouveau with everything that went before it, we can see that it expressed a new taste – one that was opulent, extravagant and yet tinged with melancholy. Here are the convoluted metal electric-light fittings, the exotically curvaceous pieces of furniture, and above all the typical svelte, moody nymphs and naiads with long flowing hair, gracefully emerging from polished wood or gleaming metal. Big stores played an important part in popularizing the new style, and the very term we now use to describe it is taken from Siegfried Bing's shop *L'Art Nouveau,* opened in Paris in 1895. Heal's became a leading purveyor of Art Nouveau wares with Ambrose Heal as chief designer; and the continuing importance of Liberty's is highlighted by the fact that the store gave its name to the style in Italy, *stile Liberty.* In these and other guises (*Jugendstil,* "youth style", in Germany, *Arte Joven,* "young art", in Spain) Art Nouveau had a double aspect, as both a serious movement in the arts and a commercialized craze.

Art Nouveau and the "decadents"
The style was also linked with the writers and artists who are sometimes grouped together as "decadents". They posed as people who had exhausted every pleasure, ruining and/or refining their sensibilities to a point at which they could appreciate only the delicately perverse and exquisitly sinful. J. K. Huysmans gave the lead in France in the 1880s, and his novel *A Rebours* was imitated in England by Oscar Wilde, whose *Portrait of Dorian Gray,* published in 1891, became a kind of textbook for the would-be decadent. Wilde, the aesthete of the 1880s, had developed into the amoral artist of the 1890s, and was soon to undergo another transformation into the popular playwright who softened his wit with sentiment. The decadent outlook was symbolized for many people by the *Yellow Book,* though it was probably the magazine's advanced design and graphic work, rather than its generally respectable content, that gave it such a sinister reputation. The art editor of the *Yellow Book* was a young man named Aubrey Beardsley, whose black and white illustrations epitomized the decadent mood: at their best they created a claustrophobic atmosphere of terrible secrets and whispered sins; at their worst they have the coy naughtiness of the schoolboy's dirty joke. The bold unshaded blacks and whites, and even some of the erotic poses, illustrate the impact of Japanese design. But the sweeping

lines, elongated figures and inverted moral atmosphere are the height of Art Nouveau decadence in England.

In Britain the decadent bubble burst with the trial and conviction of Wilde for his homosexual activities. This became the excuse for one of those outbreaks of mob righteousness of which every country learns to be ashamed, symbolized in Wilde's case by the prostitutes dancing for joy in the streets when he was sent to prison. One result of the public reaction was that Beardsley had to resign his position on the *Yellow Book*. After a brief period as editor of the *Savoy* he retired to Menton, where he died of tuberculosis in 1898, still only twenty-six years old.

Popular Art Nouveau in England and America

Despite its moral outrage, the public that bought Art Nouveau furnishings was also touched by the decadent spirit – though admittedly in a watered-down form. We can sense this *fin de siècle* spirit in the flowing lines and elongated forms of figures and decorations, though it is often hard to pin down the cause of the impression when the subject-matter seems innocuous. But when we look at the snakes, bats and lizards on posters, pottery and jewelry, there is no room left for doubt. The female figures too, with their enigmatic expression and ambiguous poses, are a long way from the complacent healthiness or sugary eroticism of the earlier Victorians. It is one of the curiosities of history that this mood, equally well marked in London, Paris and Vienna, lasted only a few years and had vanished long before the First World War.

The presence of both old and new features gives a special sort of interest to the posters of the 1890s. Poster art, pioneered by Jules Chéret, reached maturity in the works of the painters Toulouse-Lautrec and Bonnard. Bold outlines and bright colors became the norm under the influence of Japanese prints and the realization that immediate impact was of decisive importance in outdoor advertising; but in Britain and America there remained a lingering fondness for homely humorous anecdotes. Posters were, however, designed in the full Art Nouveau style, though none of them rivaled those of Adolphe Mucha in France, in which trailing hair, drapery and lettering make up an intricate, colorful mass of decorative detail. Art Nouveau and anecdote are often found together in the work of Dudley Hardy, who used flat colors and Art Nouveau lettering, but whose figures are usually conventionally realistic or comic. The "Beggarstaff Brothers" – James Pryde and William Nicholson – forged a style in which the heavy outlines and large color areas of the Japanese were combined with tonal effects that give their posters an indefinite, uniquely evocative atmosphere. In America, Ethel Reed produced highly decorative posters in a "Japanese-Art Nouveau" style, while Edward Penfield combined a modern look with an attachment to anecdote. Posters by lesser-known figures of the 1890s are surprisingly attractive, and the mixture of stylistic elements requires a certain amount of pleasurable detective-work.

Glass was one of the most effective materials for expressing the very fluid, undulating quality of Art Nouveau. The strong Art Nouveau feeling for plant and vegetable forms also found an outlet, most typically in flower-holders that were themselves in the form of flowers or large buds. On these the waved edges which had been used on glass for decades – often rather unattractively – were both elegant and appropriate. The leading British Art Nouveau glassmaker was Harry Powell, whose connection with Morris and Webb confirms the link between early British progressive design and the style of the 1890s. Powell's talent was for delicate plain or tinted glasses with long stems and bowls suggestive of flower buds. Like so many British artists, he worked in a very restrained style, avoiding the ingenuities and brilliant colors of his great French contemporary Emile Gallé. Decorative excess was a feature of a more popular market, but the objects produced often had no real point of contact with Art Nouveau. Typical of the contemporary taste for novelties were streaked and crackled glass, and also satin glass, which can be fascinating when the overall design is not outlandish. Satin glass was made by trapping air between two layers of glass;

the play of light on the air-backed transparent casing created its "padded satin" look.

American work in the applied arts assumed a far greater interest in the 1890s. The great genius of American Art Nouveau was Louis Comfort Tiffany, son of the famous jeweler. Tiffany had trained as a painter and practised as an architect before he turned to glassmaking. (Later still he took up pottery and, in the family tradition, jewelry.) His most famous work is the "Favrile" hand-blown glass, with iridescent metallic sheen and combinations of brilliant reds and yellows, browns and greens, blues and golds. Some of Tiffany's designs were flower-like, but there are also many with smooth, flowing shapes reminiscent of pottery.

"Peachblow", "Burmese" and other types of glass featuring shaded colors were also American in origin. Burmese, first made in 1886 by the Mount Washington Co. at New Bedford, Mass., was shaded from a greenish yellow into a rich pink. Later produced at Stourbridge in England, it became a favorite of Queen Victoria's, and oil-lamp shades, fairy-light shades and small candle-holders were made in "Queen's Burmese ware". Lacking the dynamic whip-lash line, it is a softened, quietly charming kind of Art Nouveau.

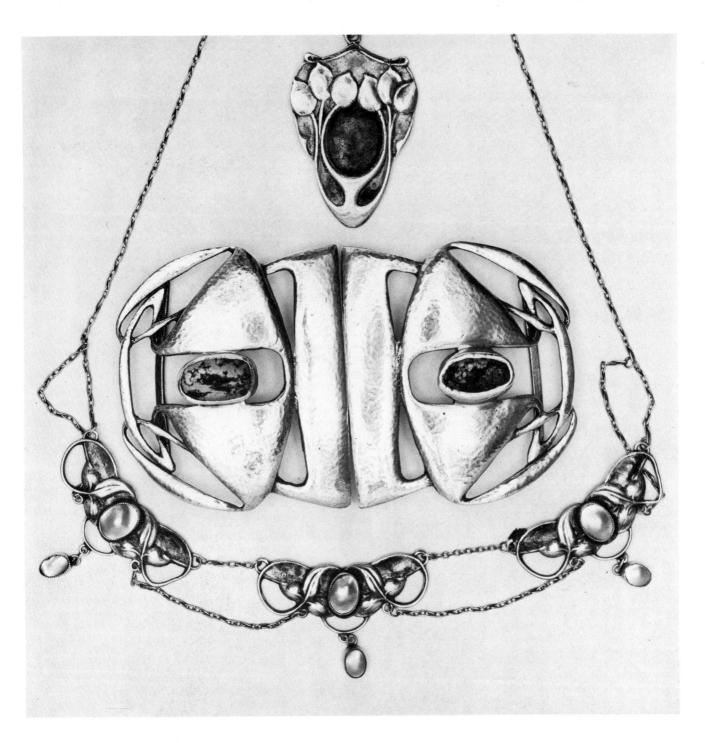

The renewed fashion for cut glass in the 1880s and 1890s was a notable countertrend to Art Nouveau. Late-19th-century cut glass was even more splendid and elaborate than at the height of its mid-century vogue, though its elaborateness was not that of Art Nouveau. Americans call this the Brilliant Period of cut glass, and the suggestion of diamonds in the term seems appropriate. Cut glass can be seen as an equivalent in upper-class tableware to expensive jewelry, in which diamonds were used for preference in "invisible" settings that displayed only the large, sparkling, beautifully cut stone. Like diamonds, cut glass represented an essentially conservative form of ostentation.

Metals were also well suited to Art Nouveau

designs, and C. R. Ashbee worked in a particularly attractive style, balancing the solid smooth body with often thread-like additions or supports. Silver sold by big firms such as Tiffany's of New York and Liberty's of London ranged from extreme examples of Art Nouveau, in which the emphasis was on decoration rather than function, to relatively conservative and utilitarian pieces. Liberty's Cymric ware was an example of Celtic design, which became very popular at the end of the century. Celtic jewelry was made by Alexander Fisher and Celtic pottery by Christopher Dresser, while commercial versions were marketed by Liberty's. The Celtic was in a sense the last of the historical revivals, but one whose curving, strap-like ornament could easily be accommodated to Art Nouveau lines. The Art Nouveau taste for metalwork led to the revived use of pewter, which had long been out of fashion except for very humble objects. The trend culminated just after Queen Victoria's death in Liberty's elegant "Tudric" pewterware, which had a high silver content and was intended as a direct substitute for the more precious metal.

On a still higher level, there is the metalwork of the four Macs. Mackintosh's ironwork for the Glasgow School of Art, like his architecture, is an idiosyncratic blend of Art Nouveau ornament and rough-textured, rectilinear structures. The Macdonald sisters had little of Mackintosh's feeling for abstract design but a splendid talent for pure Art Nouveau decoration. The dreamy sadness of the women on the sisters' copper and brass panels is a typical Art Nouveau development of the Pre-Raphaelite treatment, with a sinister touch often achieved simply by making the women stare straight at the spectator. The Macdonalds probably came closest of all British artists to the enigmatic, serpentine style so favored on the Continent.

Ceramic designs in Art Nouveau style were on the whole less successful. But there were exceptions, including those of the American Rookwood pottery, whose wares carry paintings done under a double glaze, which makes them look as though they are submerged in water. One of the most interesting examples of British Art Nouveau pottery can be seen by every shopper in London: W. J. Neatby's tile plaques (1902) in Harrod's food hall, with charmingly naïve scenes of birds and flowers.

As we have seen, this kind of two-dimensional work seems to have been more congenial to the English temperament than the rounded-out curves of French Art Nouveau. Even British sculpture in the style does not have the feelings of "presence" associated with figures in the round. The exception here was the leading sculptor Alfred Gilbert, creator of the Famous *Eros* in Piccadilly Circus. Gilbert studied in Italy and was influenced by 16th-century Italian Mannerism (which has itself some points in common with Art Nouveau); his jewelry is of particular interest because it has a heavy, fleshy look that is rare in British work. There are also many pieces of jewelry in the flatter British Art Nouveau style, though it must be admitted that none of them can compare with the splendid creations of Lalique in France.

Opposite *Buckle, necklace and pendant by Liberty's. It has the "fleshy" look characteristic of Continental rather than British Art Nouveau.*

Above *This Viennese ornament epitomises Art Nouveau, with its stylized curving plant form blossoming into a slender girl.*

Art Nouveau outlived Queen Victoria, but only by a few years. About 1905, a new simplicity and attention to function–pioneered, like Art Nouveau itself, by British artists such as Voysey–announced the controversial beginnings of 20th-century modernism. On the social level, anti-Victorianism set in quickly, encouraged by the asperities of writers like Lytton Strachey, and much of the moral and actual furniture of the preceding period was thrown out. Only in the last few years have we felt at a sufficient distance from the Victorians to sift their achievements with at least some degree of objectivity.

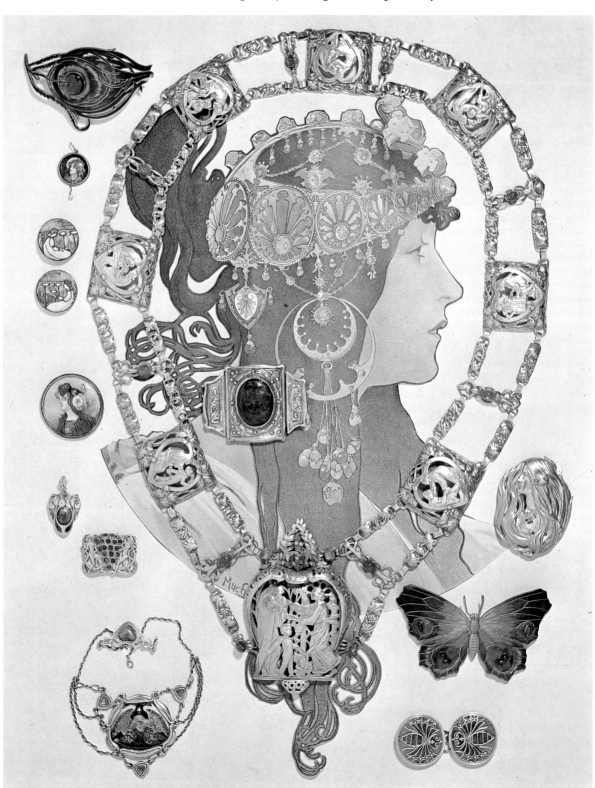

A splendid group of Art Nouveau buckles, pendants, buttons and brooches by Child and Child, Ashbee, Henry Wilson and Omar Ramsden set against a poster by Alphonse Mucha.